WHO KILLED MOOSEWALA?

WHO KILLED MOOSEWALA?

THE SPIRALLING STORY OF VIOLENCE IN PUNJAB

Jupinderjit Singh

Published by Westland Non-Fiction, an imprint of Westland Books, a division of Nasadiya Technologies Private Limited, in 2023

No. 269/2B, First Floor, 'Irai Arul', Vimalraj Street, Nethaji Nagar, Alapakkam Main Road, Maduravoyal, Chennai 600095

Westland, the Westland logo, Westland Non-Fiction and the Westland Non-Fiction logo are the trademarks of Nasadiya Technologies Private Limited, or its affiliates.

ISBN: 9789357764612

Typeset by Jojy Philip, New Delhi 110015
Printed at ...

For the fans of Sidhu Moosewala

CONTENTS

AUTHOR'S NOTE

There are a number of people I interviewed to make sure this book remained true to life—Sidhu Moosewala's parents, his friends, his former music teacher and college professors, colleagues from the Punjabi music industry, officers from the Special Cell (SC) of the Delhi Police, and the officers from the Anti-Gangster Task Force of the Punjab Police. I have tried to reconstruct the incidents of Moosewala's life and death, the police investigation into his death and the arrest of suspects, as faithfully as I could based on these interviews. Wherever possible, I have tried to provide the names of the people I spoke to. However, journalists cultivate several confidential sources over the years to aid their reporting. I, too, spoke to many such sources who agreed to speak to me only if I kept their identities confidential—the names of such sources have been withheld.

To give details regarding the police investigation and arrests of suspects, I have relied heavily on the chargesheet filed by the police in the trial court against the accused. To the best of my knowledge, these are the facts as they stand today, and until and unless they are disproved in the future, they present a true picture of the events surrounding Moosewala's death.

In order to fully understand the life of Sidhu Moosewala and to chart his growth from his image as a gun-toting rap star into a soulful singer beloved of millions, I have analysed the lyrics of some of his songs and translated some verses for ease of understanding. The use of the lyrics is minimal and solely for the purpose of comment and analysis.

I wrote this book for everyone who loved Moosewala and engaged with his music. I hope many more people discover him and his music through this book.

Jupinderjit Singh
May 2023

ONE

THE LAST RIDE

29 May 2022. It was a sultry summer evening. Punjabi rap singer Sidhu Moosewala left his home, a sprawling haveli in his village, Moosa, in his Mahindra Thar SUV. He was accompanied by his cousin Gurwinder and friend Gurpreet. The three were close. All in their late twenties, they had studied and had many an escapade together. Twenty-eight-year-old Moosewala was the only one not yet married. At six feet and three inches, the strapping young man was the tallest of the group. In stature as well, he far surpassed the other two. A rap sensation, he had amassed fame and wealth and was loved by millions of fans.

Sidhu was at the wheel and Gurwinder sat beside him. Gurpreet slipped into the rear seat. 'Guard *le ja, putt*,' Charan Kaur, Sidhu's mother, insisted. '*Nahi ta* Fortuner *le ja. Mera dil ghatda*.' (Take the guard along, son. Or go in the Fortuner. My heart sinks in fear otherwise.)

Following several threats to his life by gangsters, the Punjab government had provided four gunmen to the singer for his security. Two of the four men, however, had been inexplicably withdrawn just a day earlier, a decision that would turn out to have far-reaching consequences.

Of the two remaining police guards, one had fever and could not accompany him. Moosewala asked the other to stay back and rest since he hadn't slept much the night before. '*Bas chhoti jehi ride leni Guri te Gurwinder naal ne. Thar de pichhe jagah ghat hai chothe bande layi,*' he reportedly told the guards. (It's only a short ride in the Thar with Guri and Gurwinder. The rear seat does not have enough space for a fourth person.) To his mother he said, '*Maasi de ghar hi ja reha haan. Jyada door nahi.*' (I am only going to Maasi's house. Not too far.) He was referring to his aunt in the village of Khara Barnala about 8 km away.

His mother wanted Sidhu to take their Toyota Fortuner. It was bulletproof. The singer had spent nearly Rs 22 lakh on its modification, converting it into a tank-like fortified vehicle. The windows had 40mm thick glass to block any bullet from breaking in. Iron sheets had been added to the door frames and other places. The fuel lid was protected too, something that even bulletproof police cars often didn't have.

'Just a short *geri*, Mummy. *Sah ghutda mera andar. Tuhanu pata hi hai. Apne pind ki hona mainu?* Thar *le jaan da mann hai,*' Sidhu placated his mother. (It's a short drive. You know how caged I feel indoors. What can happen to me in my neighbourhood? Let me take the Thar today.) Charan Kaur was in a hurry. She was the village sarpanch and had to go to a neighbour's house to settle a dispute. 'Dhyan rakkhi,' she told her son and left.

If only Sidhu Moosewala had paid heed to his mother's warnings.

A CCTV camera hooked to the boundary wall of the haveli recorded the Thar leaving the house at 5.15 p.m.

'*Golgappe khawaange*,' Gurwinder recalls Sidhu whispering to them as the car left the safety of the haveli. (We will feast on golgappas.) 'Sidhu was fond of eating chaat from a shop in Mansa city. Though we had been warned not to make a habit of visiting one place regularly because of the threats,' Gurwinder would state later.

'He was humming as he drove,' Gurwinder recalled. 'We usually didn't chat much when he hummed. That was his zone of creativity.'

They had barely left the gates of the haveli when they were greeted by expectant fans. Sidhu slowed down and people thronged the SUV, clicking selfies and screaming about how much they admired the rap star. Amidst this crowd were two men, later identified as Kekda and Nikku, who took selfies with the star.[1] Nikku even walked ahead of the rolling Thar and seemed to be shooting a video on his phone.

In reality though, Nikku was not shooting a reel for Instagram or Facebook. He was on a video call with someone through the Signal app, sharing real-time intel on Moosewala's movements. Nikku would confess to this after his arrest, but the police would never recover the phone he had used. Nikku had destroyed it according to plan.

Moosewala reached the main road that connected his village to Mansa in the southeast and the Barnala town in the north. He turned west towards his aunt's village. He drove towards the sun, which was still shining brightly even as it gradually slid down towards the horizon. In an hour or so, the rays of the setting sun would form a necklace of orange light along the western horizon, illuminating and encircling the earth.

Did Moosewala think about the setting sun at all—symbolic of the end?

The rap star's twenty-ninth birthday was just fourteen days away, and his wedding about a month.

Always in a maroon turban, worn in the comfortable shahi Patiala style, Sidhu Moosewala was a symbol of hypermasculinity for his listeners and fans. He was a Jatt-Sikh from the dominant Sidhu clan. The Sidhus, according to historians, came from the Bhatti Rajputs, who descended from the Yaduvanshis of the erstwhile Rajputana sometime in the thirteenth century.[2] They moved to Punjab in the sixteenth century and settled in Bathinda. They later established the Phulkian dynasty in Patiala, Nabha, Faridkot, Malaudh and Jind. The village of Mehraj in Bathinda was their central settlement. The former chief minister of Punjab, Captain Amarinder Singh, and his forefathers belong to this village.

With the passage of time, Sidhus spread to other parts of Bathinda, including Mansa. In the modern context, the

Sidhus are referred to as the firebrand farmer community of Punjab, and at 21 per cent of Punjab's population, they are amongst the most influential ethno-religious groups in the state.

Sidhu Moosewala's music videos were often criticised for their violent content. In them, he brandished guns as luxury cars flew past in the background. The aggression and hypermasculine behaviour that he exhibited in his videos was not an entirely alien concept. In the region where he came from, it was considered a show of strength. His public persona was in line with his position in the caste and class structure of the state. His videos consolidated his image of a rebellious young man unafraid of confrontation. The singer often challenged his enemies to come face to face. 'I can surely handle many of you,' he said in a video while responding to those making threatening phone calls to him.[3]

The Thar moved along the road. Moosewala placed his pistol, a .455 bore Chrome-plated US-made Ithaca, in the accessory pocket of the driver's door. He had bought this weapon a year ago and had an arms licence to carry it. He drove past rows of keekar, tahli, neem and eucalyptus trees that lined the road on either side.

The keekar tree can survive without much water and is found all over Punjab, especially in the birs, the local name for a small forest. It is more common in Malwa, especially in the Mansa and Bathinda districts. It is a tree with its own story of resistance in Punjab, where it nearly went extinct two decades ago but then bounced back to a large extent.

Tahli or sheesham is the state tree and is grown for its wood while the neem tree is known to be a natural cleanser of the environment. The eucalyptus is the odd one in the group. A tall tree, it is almost three to four times higher than the others that remain under 15 metres. A water guzzler, the eucalyptus is often referred to as the villain of Punjab forestry. Yet, farmers and the government grow it for high returns yielded by its wood.

Beyond these trees, most of the fields that the Thar passed lay vacant. Farmers had harvested the wheat crop more than a month ago and the paddy-sowing season was still about two weeks away. Some of the fields had a layer of black soot and ash after farmers had set the wheat stubble on fire. The cheapest option for farmers to eliminate the wheat stem and roots and clear the field for the next crop, this common practice has come under much criticism in recent times. Not only does it kill the nutrients in the soil, plumes of thick smoke rising from the burnings engulf the sky and, backed by winds, travel eastwards, 300 km away, towards the national capital of Delhi. Especially towards the last months of the year, this smoke from stubble burning in Punjab adds a lethal touch to the existing smog in Delhi, leaving the residents of the city gasping for breath for weeks.

At this point though, a different kind of fire had been ignited somewhere—a fire that perhaps no one had noticed but the flames of which would soon engulf Delhi.

TWO

NOT JUST A RAP STAR

Outside the Thar's window, some fields were soft brown, while several others had a tinge of green where saplings of moong had pushed through the ground. The new chief minister of Punjab, Bhagwant Mann of the Aam Aadmi Party, had promised a minimum support price (MSP) for moong, which is an in-between pulse crop in the wheat-paddy cycle and provides natural nutrients like nitrogen to rejuvenate the fields.[1] This assurance prompted many enterprising farmers in the Mansa district to experiment with growing moong and in 2022, the district topped the state in the cultivation of the crop with 10,000 hectares under it.

Balkaur Singh, Moosewala's father had also sown the crop on a few acres. The singer had cultivated the land, riding his iconic twin-coloured tractor, an HMT 5911 model. In fact, his music label, '5911', was named after the tractor. He had even filmed songs on the yellow and orange tractor which had been modified with super speakers. Moosewala was not just a rapper; being a farmer was integral to his identity.

He had participated in the farmers' protest against the three controversial farm laws introduced by the Narendra Modi government. The new laws were said to enable an open countrywide market for the farmers to sell their crop anywhere in the country, not just in their local market. Farmers from Punjab led the nation in opposing the new laws, arguing that they did not gurantee that the government would buy their products at an MSP.

Since its introduction in the 1980s, the MSP has provided a sense of security to farmers in Punjab and has encouraged the state to become the country's food bowl. The central government introduced the new laws in September 2020 and did not budge in the face of the protests that erupted against them. In an unprecedented agitation, more than 200 farmer unions descended on the national capital in early October.[2] They came on tractors and on foot and parked themselves at the Tikri and Singhu borders, refusing to dissolve their dharna till their demands were heard. The protests continued for more than a year, till November 2021. Lakhs of farmers and supporters participated in the dharna despite the bitter Delhi cold. The protests were not without hardships. Three women from Mansa died in a road accident on 28 October while on their way home to fetch supplies for the dharna.[3] Rather than act as a deterrent, this prompted several more to join the protests. What was interesting to observe was that many a singer, actor, writer and director of the Punjabi film industry made their allegiance to the cause known. They either supported the dharna by being there or by tweeting their support on social media. They spoke from the stage, composed speeches and shot documentaries. They wrote and sang songs and stood in solidarity with the farmers.

Moosewala was among the singers who openly declared their support for the farmers' agitation. Not only had he taken his tractor all the way to Delhi, he had penned a song, *Panjab, My Motherland*, at the dharna site in Delhi. There was no doubting that Moosewala wanted to be seen as a fearless rebel, at least as far as the Indian government was concerned.

The first two stanzas of the song were enough to raise eyebrows: '*Oh Santa de hathan … Mainu Punjab kehnde aa.*'

> Nothing is comparable to the strength
> of the arrow in the hand of the saints
> Punjab is not Kashmir
> Which you will suppress
>
> Punjabis openly challenge
> Their enemies and take revenge
> If it comes to that
> They can take on Delhi anytime

With its reference to Khalistani ideologue Sant Jarnail Singh Bhindranwale, each sentence unmistakably smacked of rebellion. He followed it up with the film *Moosa Jatt*, which highlighted the plight of farmers. In the film's posters, an imposing Moosewala was seen riding his 5911 tractor skywards.[4] Little did anyone know that the same tractor would carry his body one day, in a funeral procession attended by lakhs and watched live by millions across the globe.

They had only spent a few minutes on the road when Gurwinder spotted a Bolero trailing them. 'They must be fans,' Sidhu said, used to being followed by his admirers. He didn't make much of it, turning instead towards the village of Jawaharke, which was about 8 km away from his haveli. He was only 2 km away from his maasi's house.

Gurwinder couldn't take his eyes off the vehicle still following them. 'That Bolero is still trailing us,' he said, a hint of worry in his voice. He had also noticed a Corolla behind the Bolero.

'Some fans just don't give up, do they?' Sidhu chuckled. 'Let them draw up closer and get their selfie.' Moosewala slowed down to negotiate a curve on the road as they entered the village of Jawaharke.

Gurpreet recalls asking Sidhu to turn inside the village instead of the phirni (a road circling a village). 'I don't have a good feeling about these two cars,' he told

Moosewala, looking at them. Suddenly, the Corolla sped to overtake the Bolero and came adjacent to Moosewala's Thar.

On Moosewala's right were a Ravidass temple and a two-wheeler puncture repair shop. On the left were two houses and vacant fields on both sides of the road for about 10 feet. The assailant in the Corolla had stopped the Thar just ahead of the gate of a kothi bearing the nameplate of Sardar Maluk Singh. Later, five bullets would be recovered from the front wall of that house and two others would be found embedded in the wall of the temple opposite it.

It all happened too fast.

A man in the co-passenger seat of the Corolla took out an assault rifle and opened fire from his window.

The pounding of the bullets rattled the Thar.

Moosewala grabbed his Ithaca pistol and shot six rounds at the men. Not one bullet hit them. He seemed to have tried to fight back, even though he had already been hit. In his last moments, he stayed true to the macho image he portrayed in his songs. Forensic examiners would find the used bullets later and testify to his resilience.

Meanwhile, the man with the assault rifle had darted out of the car, spraying bullets freely at the Thar. Several shots hit the windscreen and the tyres. Gurwinder and Gurpreet ducked to escape the bullets raining on them. They were not carrying any weapons.

Moosewala aimed at the shooter carrying the assault rifle, but he hadn't expected his attackers to have reinforcements. The Bolero had stopped behind the Corolla. Four men had emerged and fired at the Thar. The doors of both the vehicles were left open.

One of the assailants, who looked like a teenager, held a gun in each hand and was firing simultaneously from them. All of the attackers were armed and for several minutes, only the deafening rat-a-tat sound of gunshots and metal striking against metal, the glass and the walls behind the car could be heard. Meanwhile, the driver of the Corolla, who was still at the wheel, reversed. But the door on the passenger's side was still hanging open. As a result, it hit the open doors of the Bolero, wrecking its hinges. When the assailants sped away from the spot later, the door was still open.

A couple on a bike had moved to the edge of the road as the Corolla overtook the Thar. They had sensed something was off, but before they knew what was happening, the terrifying shooting unfolded. They dropped their motorcycle and ran to find shelter. Two other cars following the Bolero stopped and reversed in panic. CCTV footage that went viral later showed the Thar being followed by the Bolero, which was in turn followed by the Corolla just before the bend on the road in the village of Jawaharke.[5]

The bloodshed after the bend on the road was not captured on any CCTV.

The assailants ran back to their vehicles and sped away. The Corolla's damaged door was still hanging open, and the first assailant was seen holding on to it desperately. The men in the Corolla rightly surmised that the unhinged door made them too conspicuous and could leave a trail of witnesses who could help the police track them. The two shooters waited by the side of the road, stopped an Alto, threw out the unsuspecting couple who were in it and sped off, abandoning the Corolla.

Meanwhile, the other shooters in the Bolero were speeding towards their destination—a dhaba 3 km outside Mansa on the road to the neighbouring state of Haryana—when they saw a police van behind them. The Bolero turned towards an unpaved road to lose the police van. The vehicle with the cops in it went on ahead, unperturbed.

The Bolero, however, had lost its way. The attackers drove around the fields on kutcha roads for a while, fearing the police were chasing them. Finally, they abandoned the Bolero and disappeared into the tall maize crops.

The police would later discover that the four shooters had hidden for more than an hour in the village of Khyala, barely 10 km from the crime scene. The Delhi Police would mention this in their investigative report. The Punjab Police also said in their chargesheet that the shooters lost their way and hid in the fields. All the assailants could have been caught then and there if the cops had reacted differently.

In retrospect, a lot could have been done differently. Perhaps if all four of the guards of his original security detail had been with him that day, he may still have been alive. And if the police had acted swiftly, the shooters could have been caught within an hour of the crime. But then, the Punjab Police did not seal their borders with Haryana. There were no special police barricades set up to check suspects either.

Officials confess in private that some villagers had reported seeing suspicious men outside their village to the police. A Police Control Room team was sent to check. They reached the fields but said they didn't see anyone. Meanwhile, the shooters established contact with the foreign-based mastermind of the crime, who then sent a different car for them.

Left behind at the crime spot was the Thar, riddled with bullets. The imposing star of *Moosa Jatt* and the jewel of Indian hip-hop Sidhu Moosewala lay slumped in his seat, and so did his two companions. Shocked eye-witnesses and others came to help once their initial fear subsided. They pulled Moosewala out of the car. He was still breathing. The blood oozing from his gunshot wounds had turned his orange T-shirt red. His signature turban had unravelled.

The killers had sprayed around thirty bullets at the Thar. The autopsy report revealed that Moosewala had died within fifteen minutes of the first shot. Bullets, shrapnel and glass shards had caused nineteen wounds in his body.[6] Seven bullets had hit him, one had lodged in his lungs. The forensic report said bullets were fired from an AK-47 rifle, a .30 bore pistol and several 9mm pistols. One bullet from the rifle was found embedded in a tyre of the Thar.

While streaming videos and pictures shot by people around the murder spot, TV and web channels played a couplet from Moosewala's latest song, *The Last Ride*: '*Ho chobbar … janaza mithiye.*'

> The glow on this young man's face suggests
> He will be laid to rest in his youth.

THREE

THE FATHER

'I guarded the borders of India. Can't I guard my son? Of course I can. And I will.' Lying on a cot in the courtyard of his large haveli, Balkaur Singh tried to convince himself.

The palatial haveli was on the outskirts of their village, unlike their small, two-room ancestral house that stood right in its middle. Shubh, as Balkaur called his son, had only built the haveli a few months ago. 'A gift for my parents,' he had said.

Their new mansion had designer interiors. The rooms were spacious and the roof was high. The beds were large and comfortable with mattresses that were soft as bales of cotton. But for Balkaur, nothing compared to his cot, woven with ropes, on which a thin bed sheet was spread. He preferred it to all else.

It had not even been four weeks since the family had moved to its new dwelling. On 3 May, after an Akhand path of the Guru Granth Sahib, Balkaur, Charan and Shubhdeep had entered their home. Just about 300 metres from the Mansa-Talwandi Sabo road, the haveli was a far cry from their humble home near the village pond where Balkaur and Charan used to live earlier with their son. Back then, Balkaur had been in the army and Charan used to run a primary school from one of the two rooms in the house. Little Shubhdeep sat among the other village children on a mat spread on the floor, in the room or sometimes outside in the small courtyard, for his initial schooling.

On days that Balkaur was home, he would enjoy his afternoon siesta on his cot in the courtyard of the old house. Now, lying in this huge haveli, he remembered those peaceful moments. The nights had become long and tense, and peace had evaded him completely. The previous night had been particularly tough. The Punjab government had withdrawn two of the four security personnel from his son's security duty. The news had broken around 10 a.m. on 28 May and Balkaur had been stressed since then. How would only two guards protect his son round the clock? He would have to do more, Balkaur decided. He had already been up and about at night for many weeks, keeping a vigil. He was sure he could prevent any attack. However, they had been warned that assailants could attack the house armed with sophisticated weapons, grenades, even a rocket-propelled grenade launcher.

The night before, Balkaur had remained perched under a canopy on the rooftop of the haveli, peering into the dark. 'Shubh is reckless. He doesn't exercise caution while mingling with the crowd. But his guards and friends are always with him. They will protect him. *Waheguru dhyan rakhega.* And at home, I will protect him,' Balkaur continued to mutter.

If Balkaur doted on his son, Sidhu revered his father. His father's support and love meant a lot to the singer and had inspired one of his most controversial songs, *295*. Facing controversies and criticism for promoting gun culture and violence in his songs, Moosewala sang: '*Bhavein aukhi hoyi … educate milugi.*'

> No matter the crowd of critics
> No matter how harsh and hurtful their words
> Remember, just remember one thing, my son
> Your father is proud of you
>
> Mistaken are those who think you have fallen
> Get up, my ox-like son
> Keep telling the truth through your songs
> The educated audience in the future will understand you

Shubhdeep Singh Moosewala had only started singing professionally five years ago, but his popularity had spiked faster than that of other singers. His income tax returns were proof of his meteoric rise.

In 2017–18, his income was a little more than Rs 5 lakh. In 2018–19, it increased to Rs 25 lakh, and then spiked to over a crore in 2019–20. By 2020–21 his income had almost doubled to Rs 3 crore. In May 2022, the month Moosewala was murdered, he was estimated to be worth more than Rs 100 crore. Moosewala's financial manager, Bunty Bains, a lyricist and producer, pegged the value of his songs at more than Rs 500 crore after his death.

Balkaur Singh had 6 acres of land of his own, his share of the family farmland. His son added another 40 acres to it, besides gifting a tractor to his mother. He planned to buy another 25 acres in the village in the coming years.

Sidhu Moosewala's career was on a sharp incline. His song *So High* had crossed 305 million views. In 2018, PTC Punjabi Music Awards nominated him in the Best New Age Sensation category for his song *Issa Jatt*. He won the Best Album Award at the 2019 Brit Asia TV Music Awards (BAMA), his song *47* featured in the top 20 on the UK mainstream weekly and New Zealand Hot 40 charts. Many more accolades followed.

In later interviews, Balkaur would wonder out loud if his son had fallen victim to the evil eye of ill-intentioned people. But back then, his success had only been cause for celebration.

⸻

Balkaur looked around the house to reassure himself. Strong searchlights beamed atop the minarets in the corners. Two cops stood at the main doors which were about 14 feet high and made of teak. Shubh had got them specially carved and ornamented. Balkaur made a mental note to check on the guards the next day and ensure that they got some rest.

Shera and Baghera, Shubh's beloved dogs, paced around the courtyard. With keen senses and teeth sharp like a commando's knife, the Dobermanns were trained to rip out an intruder's flesh instantly. Shubh often fed them with his hands. For days after his murder, the dogs wouldn't eat anything.

Balkaur remembered the initial days of his army life. Back then, nothing missed him. Whether it was the swift movement of a rat or a rabbit in the bushes, the quick slithering away of a snake or the falling of a leaf in the dark—his sharpened senses caught everything. Age hadn't affected his alertness. Surely he could spot an assailant if the need arose, he assured himself.

Balkaur had a fixed everyday routine. After his self-assigned extended guard-duty at night, he slept for a few hours in the morning. He would leave the house early to attend to the crops or would go to the Mansa fire station where he was posted as a fireman. The last month had been busy for the fire fighters. The auspicious day of Baisakhi in April signalled the beginning of the month of harvesting. Farmers and their families would take a dip in the pond near the village Gurdwara and seek blessings for a bountiful harvest. But for the fire brigade, harvesting meant more fires to put out. They had to constantly be on the lookout, to douse the many farm fires deliberately started by the farmers to eliminate the wheat stubble.

Without the hustle-bustle of the April crop fires, the Mansa firemen usually remained free after 15 May. So Balkaur would return early and enjoy his afternoon siesta. But not before he checked with the guards and his son.

Shubhdeep's fame was spreading, but as his fanbase grew, the number of his detractors multiplied too. A few days earlier, he had gone live on YouTube, challenging those making threatening calls to him. In the live recording, Moosewala could be seen driving his Fortuner, wearing a parna around his head. He spoke into the camera about the threatening calls he had been receiving. Some of these calls were supposedly made by his music rivals and their supporters. In his video, Moosewala declared that he was not afraid of such tactics, and had nothing to be scared of. He remarked, 'I have never said anything bad about anyone behind their back. I don't indulge in such things … I say things openly, thumping my chest.' *What did those threatening Shubhdeep want?* wondered Balkaur. *Money, of course. And they want us to submit. We will do neither.*

Balkaur was proud of his son, who was a self-made star. He wrote his own songs, composed the music and sang the tracks. He would upload two or even four songs every month. The fans loved his work and his following grew steadily. He crushed any competition he had. Naturally, this rankled the music industry—the distributors as well as his rivals. One of them, Balkaur suspected, was behind these calls.

In August 2020, Moosewala launched '5911', a label meant to be a platform for budding singers to launch their songs. Shubh's plan was to help newer artists produce music without charging them. In fact, in some cases, he paid for the entire process. Not only that, he would use his fame and following to promote new talent. Balkaur believed this was his son's way of giving back to the industry that had made him a star. With such clean intentions, why should Shubh submit to threats?

In his video, Sidhu had said, 'Come face to face with me. Don't hide behind fake or anonymous profiles on social media. Only cowards issue threats.' And Sidhu Moosewala was no coward.

Balkaur admired Sidhu's guts, but admonished him often. After all, that is what any father would do, he felt. Criticise your son for his betterment and safety but admire his fearlessness in your heart. Balkaur said in an interview after Sidhu's killing that he was proud his son had a warrior's heart and a soldier's gut. 'He stood up to the sharks in the music world and to those who were threatening him. I would sometimes tell him to let barking dogs bark.'

Despite his rebellious, macho persona, Shubhdeep had always been down to earth and obedient. When he started classes in the Vidya Bharti school, Balkaur would drop him there on his scooter before starting his morning shift at the fire station. Sometimes he would get late to work after dropping little Shubhdeep to school. One day, the chief fireman chided Balkaur in front of others for never being on time. Balkaur conveyed the unpleasant news to his son: it was becoming difficult for him to manage his work schedule along with the duty of dropping Shubh off. Shubhdeep took the news stoically. If his father was finding it difficult to drop him, he would find a way to ease his burden. Merely ten years old, he began cycling to school. For Balkaur, his son would always remain that soft-spoken, considerate boy, no matter how big a star he became.

Recently, Balkaur had got into an argument on social media on Shubhdeep's behalf. The audio of it can still be found on YouTube. Though Balkaur maintains that he is against acts of violence, even the verbal kind, he felt he couldn't stay quiet when it came to his and his son's honour.

Another instance arose when he spotted some derogatory comments on a post by Moosewala. The post was a song he had recently recorded and the comments were abusive and threatened the singer. Balkaur recognised one commentator as being from a nearby village. So, he got his number and gave him a piece of his mind. He told his father off as well. 'Teach some good values to your son. This is not how he should talk to elders; he should not write abusive language on someone's Facebook and YouTube pages,' Balkaur said.

The man, also furious, unleashed more abuses and threats. Balkaur lost his cool.

'Everyone is a lion in their own den. Come out of your hiding place and meet me if you are that brave. Or tell me where I should come. For my son and I are lions. And I am young enough to take on anyone for his protection,' he roared on the phone.

Lost in these thoughts, Balkaur dozed off. A few minutes later, he heard the sound of the Thar engine and woke up with a start.

That's our Thar. Is Shubh going somewhere? Has he taken the guards with him?

'Why didn't you go with him? That vehicle is not bulletproof. How could you allow him to take that car?' Balkaur shouted at the guards and everyone around, while running towards the gate.

He was anxious. It was not the first time Shubh had broken security protocol, but today, his heart was restless. 'Sardar saab, we were about to follow him in the Fortuner,' one of the guards said. 'But the car's rear tyre was low on air pressure. So, we asked Sidhu-ji to wait and take us along. But he didn't listen. He insisted it was only a short ride.'

Balkaur yelled at the guards to get into the car immediately and sped after his son. 'He stopped outside the gate to take some selfies with fans,' one of the guards said as the car lurched out of the gates.

'Fans? Selfies? It's too dangerous,' Balkaur mumbled. 'Shubh feels stifled if he has to stay indoors for even a day. He wants to move about freely and won't listen to anyone. Only I can rein him in. He saw that I was asleep and ventured out. This boy ...'

In the First Information Report (FIR) filed by him, Balkaur mentioned that as he tried to catch up with Moosewala's Thar, he saw a Corolla and a Bolero following it. He claimed he saw eight persons, four in each car. Later, the number of assailants was determined to be six.

When he first heard the gunshots, his heart sank. The dread that had been lurking in his mind spread to his body, and he felt his hands and feet go cold. The Thar had just turned the bend in Jawaharke, followed by the two cars, and the unmistakable rat-a-tat of an assault rifle rocked everyone.

'That is an assault rifle,' a guard shouted.

'Speed up!' Balkaur said.

What Balkaur saw next was a sight no father should ever have to see.

He narrated the scene in the FIR.

'Several persons were firing at my son's Thar. It seemed to be a scene from a video game where gunshots fly freely. The assailants ran towards their cars and sped away ...'

Balkaur would later narrate to reporters how shocking it had been for him. 'My son, my tall, muscular son, whom we had nurtured with pure butter and ghee, was slumped in the Thar's seat. His head was hanging down on his chest, his turban loose on his lap. There was blood everywhere. Most of the bullets had hit the right side of his body. We pulled him out of the car. People had gathered by then. Gurwinder and Gurpreet were lying in their seats, but they responded to our shrieks. My son did not.

'Doctors at the Mansa Civil hospital declared him dead on arrival. After the postmortem, they said the first few bullets had hit his right shoulder, another one had struck his left knee, which is usually raised higher than the other while driving as one operates the clutch with the left foot. Yet another bullet had pierced his lungs through his broad chest and ribs. A solid and towering young man reduced to a heap of flesh, bones and blood-soaked clothes. My son Shubhdeep Singh Moosewala …

'What was his fault … that day, he just wanted to go out for a half-hour or so. He was at home the whole day, and the previous day too. He said he was suffocated. Needed fresh air. Just a ride …'

The last ride.

The word 'viral' assumed new proportions as the news of Sidhu Moosewala's death broke on the internet. Video clips and photos from the crime scene taken by passersby, eyewitnesses and journalists flooded every website.

Online news portals and channels almost crashed due to the sheer volume of people trying to verify the news.

This was only to be expected; his fan following was enormous.

On Twitter, Moosewala had 16 lakh followers; on Facebook, a few hundred short of 3 lakh. And on YouTube, the primary bread and butter for singers, he had a whopping 1.60 crore subscribers.[1]

As the news was confirmed, shock turned to horror and many of Moosewala's fans rushed to his house to have their hero's last darshan. First, they visited the civil hospital where his corpse was kept, and then they thronged the haveli. The crowd soon turned into a river in spate, and then grew into a sea of mourners.

At the funeral on 31 May, Balkaur stood on his son's tractor-trolley, ready for the solemn procession. Moosewala lay under flowers and garlands. The bereaved father took his turban in his hands and held it towards the crowd of mourners attending his son's funeral. Then he bowed to the lakhs of admirers who had arrived to share his sorrow that day.

When Balkaur consigned his son to the flames, he was moved to see how many seemed to mourn with him. His son returned to the elements that made him, but not before leaving an impression in the minds of so many people.

May another Shubhdeep Singh Moosewala take birth soon. Unfortunately, this one left too early, he beseeched God.

FOUR

THE THREATS

Sidhu Moosewala's death on 29 May 2022 rocked the nation. His fans, shaken to the core, could not believe their rap idol—a young man at the top of his career—was suddenly no more. But for those close to the singer, the attack was not a bolt from the blue. In fact, there had been several warning signs. What was unclear was the shape the attacks would take. Perhaps assailants would try to injure and subdue him; pass it off as a warning? Maybe the assault would be in the shape of an acid attack. Poisoning was a strong possibility too. Not to result in death necessarily, but in a way that would badly affect the rap star's voice. After all, his voice was his life.

The unspoken fear was that 'they' *could* murder him. If for no other reason than to make a grand spectacle of it.

Various security and intelligence agencies of India had been aware of such threats. The Delhi Police Special Cell, which keeps tabs on criminal elements in North India, got to know about the plans to eliminate Moosewala through a chance discovery. In April 2022, the Special Cell arrested a gangster called Shahrukh from Delhi, in connection with various cases of murder and extortion. During his interrogation, he revealed that in December 2021, a big task had been assigned to him.[1] Lawrence Bishnoi and Goldy Brar had asked him to eliminate Sidhu Moosewala. Shahrukh had closely observed the singer's routine for five days and done multiple recces in Moosa. However, intimidated by the constant presence of fans and the strong security arrangements around the singer, he aborted the plan. He would need guns with a long shooting range, he informed Bishnoi. Before he could come up with another plan, he was arrested. Investigation reports reveal that Shahrukh reported to the gangsters that either a sniper with a telescope gun could do the job, or a group of shooters would have to waylay Moosewala or even storm his house.

The Punjab Police, under whose jurisdiction Moosewala's native village fell, also had knowledge of the threats the singer was receiving. In February 2021, almost fifteen months before the singer's death, officials with the Organised Crime Control Unit (OCCU) of the Punjab Police held a meeting with the singer at their Intelligence Headquarters in Mohali, for a special briefing. Like any state police in India, the Punjab Police has different wings or cells for responding to specific crimes. The prime job of OCCU is to keep an eye on gangsters and carry out operations against them.

The OCCU officials told Moosewala that there was a real threat to his life. They had definite information that several groups of gangsters had been tasked with killing the singer. They assigned him four police guards for his personal protection and advised that he never venture out alone. One senior police official who was part of the meeting commented after Moosewala's killing, 'He was also told not to get too close to his fans, who were known to swarm around him.' Five months later, in July 2021, OCCU officials upgraded Moosewala's security cover to twelve gunmen after a fresh assessment was made of threats to his life, based on the regrouping of some gangs.

In November 2021, the number of security guards went up to eighteen. This was because Sidhu Moosewala had donned the cap of a politician. Just a few months ahead of the Punjab Assembly elections, Moosewala joined the Indian National Congress, whose government was in power in the state. The then Punjab Congress President, Navjot Singh Sidhu, was enthusiastic about the hip-hop superstar's entry into the party. 'Welcome to the fold champ,' he tweeted.[2] Moosewala's security cover now included not just the gunmen but also cops from Mansa. This enabled him to mingle with his fans more freely. Earlier, they had been just his fans, but now they were a potential vote bank. He needed to mix with them to get elected. Ironically, the Congress government had slapped four criminal cases against Moosewala earlier for promoting gun culture and violence through his songs and also for hurting religious sentiments.[3] The same government now wanted to protect him at any cost.

—•••—

The one person who knew about the threats to Moosewala's life even before the Special Cell did was the singer himself. In September 2019, he received the first-ever call for extortion. The caller identified himself as Jaggu Bhagwanpuria and demanded Rs 50 lakh as protection money. Everyone in Punjab knew that name. A Punjab Police dossier on Bhagwanpuria, prepared by IG Kunwar Vijay Pratap, listed the gangster's life, criminal record, network with other gangs and political patronage. He was among the most dreaded gangsters of the state and had enjoyed the patronage of both the Shiromani Akali Dal (SAD) and the Congress party at different times.

Moosewala ignored the call—Rs 50 lakh was a lot of money and the singer was not convinced that the call was genuine. He dismissed it as a prank. At the back of his mind was also the thought that if he paid once, he would have to keep paying. That is how the extortion racket worked.

As luck would have it, Bhagwanpuria never followed up on that call. But a few months later, Moosewala received another call. This time it was from another gangster, Harry Chatha of Amritsar, who made a similar demand.

Moosewala ignored that call too. Then, the master of all these gangsters, Lawrence Bishnoi called. This time the 'protection money' was pegged at Rs 1 crore.

Moosewala ignored it yet again.

Not just the Punjab Police, even the police of the neighbouring state of Haryana had been aware of the plots to assassinate Moosewala. They had been actively protecting him for some time. This was not common. Police of one state do not post one of their own in another state's jurisdiction unless there is a full understanding of the issue between the two states and the central security agencies. In the case of Sidhu Moosewala, however, it was deemed necessary. After joining the Congress party, Moosewala contested elections from the Mansa Assembly seat, which was his home district. Mansa bordered Haryana, which made it easy for any group to launch an assault there and then flee to Haryana or even Rajasthan. The elections were scheduled for 20 February 2022.

On 19 January, a shoot-out took place in Ambala, Haryana, where a gangster named Mohit Rana was killed. The Haryana Special Task Force (STF) arrested Raju Basodi and Kala Rana, both close aides of Lawrence Bishnoi. During their interrogation, the STF found that the same gang was contracted to target Moosewala. It assessed the threat to be serious enough to deploy cops in plainclothes to provide security to the Punjabi hip-hop star.

The STF Haryana also handed over photos of the four suspected shooters to Moosewala and his family.

The singer was told to stay vigilant and look out for these faces in the crowd. Fans often approached him for autographs or selfies. He was told not to let anyone get too close.

'How will I seek votes then?' Moosewala asked the cops. 'I have to mingle with the masses to earn their trust and votes. I will have to accept flowers or food if they offer it.'

The security order remained strict. The threats were serious and he just could not take the risk. He would have to distance himself. In an interview with Pro Punjab TV journalist Yadwinder Singh Karfew on 9 December 2021, Moosewala revealed that some people had gifted him a turban wrapped in a piece of cloth. 'I was on the way to my fields on my tractor when I met some fans. One of them handed over a packet, saying it was a turban he had got for me as a gift. I took it and kept it on the side of my seat. Later, when I was handing over the packet to my mother, I noticed something solid in it. I kept it aside and called the police. A bomb disposal squad found a contraption of wires attached to a metal object. They told me it would have been enough to cause shrapnel injuries, even fatal, to anyone who might have opened the packet.'[4]

The singer didn't want to be a sitting duck. He had bought a .455 bore, chrome-plated, US-made Ithaca pistol for self-defence. He had also placed an order for bulletproof vests. After the turban-bomb incident, he modified his Toyota Fortuner into a tank-like, fortified vehicle.

Balkaur Singh Sidhu, who had served in the Armoured Corps, was most worried about the threats to his son's life. His hearing had been impaired years ago when a tank he had been riding had met with an accident at a battlefield drill. But his senses, especially to smell out, see or sense danger, were intact, maybe even sharper.

He would often lecture the guards protecting Sidhu about remaining vigilant, and give examples from his experience in the Indian Army. 'A soldier guarding the borders can't even wink lest he miss any suspicious movement. A bullet or a mortar shell can come out of nowhere if you are deployed as a sentry on the border with Pakistan,' he would tell them.

Moosewala's friends, cousins and music colleagues also knew about the threats. After all, everyone associated with the Punjabi music industry had heard about such 'threats' or had had first-hand experience. A famous singer and actor, Parmish Verma, was shot at and wounded on 14 April 2018, late at night in Mohali. Actor Gippy Grewal, among the top Punjabi artists and singers, had lodged an FIR against threats by gangsters who wanted him to pay protection money or face a bullet like Parmish.[5] Several other artists, producers, writers and singers either paid or took police protection.

On 10 March 2022, the results of the Punjab Assembly elections were announced. The Aam Aadmi Party (AAP) led by its national president and Delhi Chief Minister Arvind Kejriwal, with Bhagwant Mann as the chief ministerial candidate, stormed to power in Punjab. The party won ninety-two out of the 117 seats. Moosewala lost the elections.

On the morning of 28 May, the Punjab government withdrew or pruned the security cover of 424 VVIPs and VIPS. Two of the four men from Moosewala's security detail were also withdrawn despite the fact that there were justified and known threats to his life.

A day later, Moosewala was dead.

In the verses of his song *The Last Ride*, Moosewala compared his life, controversies and enemies to his idol, American rap singer Tupac Shakur. In several media interviews and while performing on stage, Moosewala recalled the deep impression Shakur's songs had left on him. 'I have listened to his songs since I can remember,' he said once. In June 1996, Shakur had been riding his car in Las Vegas when he was shot by a suspected gangster. In the end, Moosewala met the same end as his music idol. Had he ever had an inkling about how similar their lives would turn out to be?

FIVE

LAWRENCE BISHNOI

In his FIR, Balkaur mentioned one name—Lawrence Bishnoi. His suspicion was based on the many threatening phone calls Moosewala had received from Bishnoi's gang. But then there were others too. Sidhu had entered into open arguments and confrontations with people on social media. Some of these people were also singers and, according to father and son, motivated by jealousy. There was also the possibility that Moosewala's political rivals had eliminated him.

About three-and-a-half hours after the murder, without any arrests or substantial evidence, the head of the Punjab Police, DGP V.K. Bhawra, the man who led some 80,000 police personnel, said the murder was due to an ongoing war between different gangs in Punjab. Balkaur Singh contested the claim. It was only the second month of the newly-formed Aam Aadmi Party's government in Punjab, and all departments were under pressure to perform or respond swiftly to any exigency. Bhawra seemed to be trying to control public anger about the murder by announcing that the police were going to catch the killers as soon as the motive was clear.

Angry fans of the singer had already crowded Mansa civil hospital, shouting slogans and demanding justice. The police also claimed that the Bishnoi gang had killed Moosewala to avenge the killing of gangster-turned-politician Vicky Middukhera, who was killed on 7 August 2021. Their reference was to Shaganpreet Singh, once Moosewala's manager and the main conspirator in Middukhera's murder.

The 'swift' police investigation was based on a Facebook post by one Goldy Brar, an A-listed, wanted gangster said to be hiding in Canada, and a key aide of Lawrence Bishnoi. In the post Goldy Brar claimed the responsibility for the killing of Moosewala. 'I, Goldy Brar, assert here that I, along with Lawrence Bishnoi and Sachin Bishnoi, have got singer Sidhu Moosewala killed. He was killed because he played a big role in the murder of our brothers Vicky Middukhera and Gurlal Brar.'[1] Brar, and later Lawrence, would also refer to the role of Shaganpreet in Vicky Middukhera's murder case. Balkaur Singh denied his son's involvement with Shaganpreet, even denying that Shaganpreet was his son's manager.

Sitting next to his son's body lying motionless on a stretcher in the civil hospital, Balkaur desperately needed some consolation, some answers, some hope. 'It is not just a crime against us but against the state,' he wailed.

Balkaur didn't believe that his son was involved in any man's killing. He criticised the insensitivity of the Punjab DGP and the state government for calling his son a gangster. The DGP apologised the next day, and so did the chief minister of Punjab. But the questions on the killing remained.

'Lawrence Bishnoi will have all the answers. Police should question him first before jumping to conclusions. My son was killed by gangsters as he refused to toe the line drawn by them, not because of a gang war!' Balkaur Sidhu shouted in agony at reporters who pressed him for a response to statements made by the police.

Before Lawrence Bishnoi became a household name, making regular appearances in the news for his nefarious exploits, India had been familiar with the Bishnoi community for very different reasons. Followers of the fifteenth-century saint, Shri Jambeshwarji, the Bishnois are known to be staunch wildlife conservationists. They live by twenty-nine principles (their name is a derivative, the 'bees-noi'), all of which are geared towards peaceful and harmonious living with nature. Not only are the Bishnois strict vegetarians, they are also forbidden from killing animals even in self-defence. For the Bishnois, wildlife is sacred and they protect it at all costs. Even dry deadwood is not burnt without carefully examining it for traces of any living organism that may have made it its home.

The Bishnois garnered national attention when in 1998, members of the community gave chase to actor Salman Khan when he was out for a hunt on their protected land, while on the outdoor location for the shoot of the movie *Hum Saath-Saath Hain*. The actor and some of his friends, also from the film industry, were reported for the shooting of chinkaras and blackbucks. In the long legal battle that ensued, several witnesses turned hostile or went missing.[2] However, two eyewitnesses, Poonam Chand Bishnoi and Chogaram Bishnoi, residents of the village of Kankani at Bagdonki Dhaani, steadfastly stood by their statements against Khan, leading to his conviction.[3] More than twenty years have passed since the incident and Khan is out on bail, but the community continues to pursue the case against the superstar and wants him to be punished for what they perceive to be sacrilege.

Standing up to protect the environment is an integral part of being a Bishnoi. It is said that in 1730, as many as 363 Bishnois, led by Amrita Devi, laid down their lives to protect a grove of Khejri trees in village of Khejarli, in modern-day Jodhpur district, from the Mewar army. This brave act has been a major influence on the modern-day Chipko movement.

Today, Bishnois are settled across Punjab, Rajasthan and Haryana. A larger concentration of the community is in the Fazilka district of Punjab, with Abohar being the main town. The Abohar Wildlife Sanctuary, at the centre of this belt, is a safe haven for the Bishnois' sacred blackbuck. At the edge of this sanctuary is village of

Duttranwali, where Lawrence Bishnoi was born on 12 February 1992.

—⊷⊶—

Just about five-and-a-half feet tall but sturdy in build, Lawrence has the looks of a film star. As per the profile dossiers on him made by the police teams of Punjab, Haryana, Rajasthan and Delhi, Lawrence is fastidious about his workout. His biceps and triceps, deltoids, trapezius and dorsal muscles appear well-defined over a broad wrestler's chest. He follows a strict free-weight exercise regimen besides working out with bodyweights in the akhara. The dossiers say Lawrence is a Brahmachari who mostly wears a langot and spends up to eight hours in dhyan or meditation. Sometimes, it was said, he would sit in meditation in his cell in Tihar Jail at midnight and get up well past sunrise. Some police officials say, on the condition of anonymity, that his deep-set eyes have the ability to scan a person thoroughly with just one look.

Why did this fresh-faced and charismatic youth turn to a world of crime? Well, it certainly wasn't for money. Lawrence's family is one of the wealthiest in the village. They live in a big haveli and own about 110 acres of land. His father, Lavinder Singh, did not study beyond class 8 and was happy managing the land. His mother, Sunita, a resident of the village of Jyotanwali near Dabwali in Haryana, was a homemaker despite being a graduate. Lavinder and Sunita had two sons, the elder one was called Lawrence and the younger, Anmol.

Both are prime accused in the Moosewala murder case.

⁂

Before his name appeared in the Moosewala case, Lawrence had already been in the news. In January 2018, he was produced in a Jodhpur court by the police for a case of extortion and for making death threats to Salman Khan. He announced to the waiting media, 'Salman Khan will be killed here, in Jodhpur ... Then he will come to know about our real identity.'[4]

Six months later, on 6 June, Lawrence's close aide Sampat Nehra was arrested by the Haryana Police. On being interrogated, he told the police that he had conducted a recce of Salman Khan's house, followed his movements and clicked several photos of the actor. Nehra said he was following Lawrence Bishnoi's directions. His task was to eliminate Salman for the blackbuck killings.

There is no doubt that in just a few years, Lawrence had emerged as a powerful gangster who could openly threaten even big stars like Khan. Fifty-two-year-old Ramesh Bishnoi, who is related to Lawrence's extended family, claims the police have painted him as a monster, which he is not.

President of the All India Jeev Raksha Bishnoi Sabha, Ramesh was forthcoming while speaking about Lawrence. Though Lawrence and he had more than twenty years between them, they were 'dada-bhai', said Ramesh. 'My grandfather and Lawrence's grandfather were brothers. Lawrence['s] family is the wealthiest … But both their sons are facing criminal cases and there does not seem to be a way back now,' he lamented.

Ramesh further spoke about how Lawrence's unusual first name had been chosen by his mother, Sunita. He was named after Henry Montgomery Lawrence, the British military officer who set up the famous Lawrence School in Sanawar. 'Lawrence she called him as he was pinkish-white like the British … she hoped her son would become a big name like Henry Lawrence, who had set up the school on the hills in Himachal Pradesh, strictly for the elite and classy,' Ramesh reminisced.

While his mother may have nurtured such dreams, the son turned out to be a nightmare for many. He set up a chain of gangs and left a trail of blood wherever he went.

From Ramesh's account and by reading police dossiers of different states, one can piece together the life of Lawrence Bishnoi before he burst on the scene as a hardened criminal. He studied till class 12 in a convent school in Abohar, about 9 km from his village. Lawrence was a good student and had, at one time, even earned a scholarship, not that he needed one. Ramesh reveals, 'Lawrence used to go in a van to the school with other kids but after class 8, he went on his own bike. And he loved branded clothes. It was no big deal for him to wear shoes worth more than Rs 10,000. He still maintains that style. Also, he used to help children of poor families in the village. It was common for him to bring the needy home, asking his parents to help. He was an introverted guy but he always had a following in the village and the school.'

After finishing school in 2008, Lawrence attended DAV College, Chandigarh, where he took a fancy to student politics. 'Lawrence had money, style and guts. It was easy for him to get followers among students, many of whom could not afford his lifestyle. Perhaps egged on by followers, he joined SOPU—Student Organisation for Panjab University—in the very first year of college,' a Chandigarh police DSP, who had arrested Lawrence after a college brawl revealed. The DAV College was affiliated to Panjab University. Every year, in September–October, elections to student organisations in the college and the university would take place. Lawrence contested these elections in 2009 but lost. It appears the loss did not go down well with the young student leader. 'Maybe he was not used to opposition, or it could be mere misfortune that he got involved in brawls over the student elections,' recollects another police officer who had questioned Lawrence in his first case.

Trusted sources in the police say that, according to police dossiers, Lawrence moved in the company of former student leaders Jaswinder Singh Rocky, Vicky Middukhera, Goldy Brar and Sampat Nehra (whom Lawrence later tasked with killing Salman Khan) in college. These people had a major impact on his life. Ultimately, the early connections that Lawrence forged made him who he is and perhaps even led to the killing of Sidhu Moosewala.

After losing the elections, Lawrence and members of the SOPU had regular heated exchanges. Ugly brawls became common and it is alleged that Lawrence once set a rival's car on fire in anger. In April 2010, after another such exchange, Lawrence and his friends were arrested. However, these fights seemed to strengthen his public standing, for in the next session, Lawrence was appointed the head of the SOPU. His strongman image was further consolidated when, in October 2010, Lawrence and his friends opened fire at yet another brawl.

Amongst all the connections Lawrence Bishnoi made during his time in Punjab student politics, his friendship with Vicky Middukhera was perhaps the strongest. The soft-spoken and unassuming Middukhera had taken young Lawrence under his wing and helped him establish his position in Chandigarh student politics. Over the years, their friendship grew so strong that Bishnoi considered Middukhera his elder brother. Vicky Middukhera would go on to become a leader of the Youth Akali Dal, while Lawrence's name gradually started gaining more importance in the underworld. His time in jail rewarded him with more criminal connections and that, coupled with his daring nature, led him to embrace a brazen life of crime. Today, he has fifty-nine criminal cases against him in Punjab, Haryana, Rajasthan and New Delhi.

In the biggest of these cases Delhi Police slapped the stringent Maharashtra Control of Organised Crime Act, 1999 (MCOCA) on Lawrence and his gangster friend, Jaggu Bhagwanpuria.[5] The MCOCA, as the name suggests, was enacted by the Maharashtra government to combat gangs and mafia that mushroomed in the state, and especially in Mumbai. The Act allows the imprisonment of gangsters and mafia men, who are recognised as dangerous to society, without trial for up to 180 days, unlike the standard 24 hours. The Act also provisions that confessions before a police officer are admissible before a court of law.

The Ministry of Home Affairs adopted MCOCA in February 2002. Punjab had similar plans but the state's political parties have not agreed to its implementation yet. Lawrence was booked under MCOCA in 2021, in Delhi, after he established a syndicate, along with gangsters and shooters of Delhi NCR (National Capital Region), which includes Noida, Gurgaon, Faridabad and Ghaziabad. The syndicate also had connections and influence in other areas in the states of Haryana, Rajasthan and Uttar Pradesh. It grew in power through networking and by cultivating supporters, sympathisers and followers across the country.

On 29 May, at about 6.30 p.m., a mobile phone rang in Delhi's Tihar Jail. The phone belonged to Lawrence's co-inmate, a gangster from New Delhi. The call was made through the Signal app, as police later discovered.

Sixty-four days later, the conversation that took place that day came to light after it was 'leaked' to the press.

THE CALL

The phone rings three times and is then answered.

Caller: Hello.

Receiver: Hello.

Caller: Hello.

Receiver: Hello. *Hanji. Ji.*

Caller: Mmmmm. *Baat ho sakti hai?* (Is it possible to speak?)

Receiver: *Haan. Bilkul ho sakti hai.* (Yes, of course, why not.)

Caller: *Karwana. Zaruri hai.* (Please connect us. It is important.)

Receiver: *Hanji. Ek* minute. (Yes. Just a moment.)

Caller: *Haanji. Thoda zaruri hai. Aise hi rakhein.* (Yes. It's a bit important. Don't disconnect.)

Receiver: *Haan. Line te rahi. Hold kari.* (Stay on the line and hold.)

A twenty-seven-second-long pause follows, during which footsteps and breathing can be heard. It seems the person holding the mobile phone is walking towards someone. When a voice is heard again, it is someone else. Police say it was Lawrence who took over the call.

Receiver: Hello?

Caller: (Inaudible. Says something like a salute to the Gurus, then continues.) *Speaker on taan ni? Meri gal sun. Mubarakan bahot, bahot bhra nu. Giani charra ta gaddi.* (I hope the speaker is not on. Listen to me. Many congratulations to you, my brother. Giani has been mowed down.)

Lawrence: *Ki?*
Caller: *Giani charra ta gaddi.*
Lawrence: *Hein?*
Caller: *Giani charra ta gaddi.*
Lawrence: *Ki karta!* (What are you saying?)
Caller: Oh, *Giani charra ta gaddi. Moosewala maar ta.* (Giani has been mowed down. Moosewala is dead.)
Lawrence: *Changa.*
Caller: Hmm ... *Ji*
Lawrence: *Maarta?*
Caller: *Haan, haan* ... hmmm
Lawrence: Ok. Cut *de.*

An hour after Moosewala's death, Bishnoi's key aide Goldy Brar wrote a post on Facebook, claiming responsibility for the murder. The post went viral worldwide—the dubious fame every gangster craves. A day later, the Punjab Police issued a look-out notice against Brar, who, according to their records, was hiding somewhere in Canada. They informed the Ministry of Home Affairs to initiate the extradition procedure with the Canadian government for the gangster's return to India. So far, Brar has not returned.

SIX

THE KILLERS

MANPREET SINGH

Kill. Kill. Kill. I will kill them all.

Manpreet Mannu, also known as Mannu Kusa, or simply Mannu, of village of Khosa in Nihal Singh Wala, Moga, would chant these words when a shot of 'chitta' or heroin took over his mind. *I will kill these upper-caste bullies*, he would think of the men who had been harassing him.

Mannu's family, who were Dalits, had embraced Sikhism a few generations ago and were now Sehajdhari Sikhs. Sehajdhari Sikhs do not wear the five symbols of Sikhism—kesh, kara, kanga, kachera and kirpan—that Amritdhari Sikhs do. Mannu, for instance, was a 'cut-surd' and had shorn off his hair. While many Dalits converted to Sikhism, perhaps in a bid to escape the rigid

Hindu caste system, it wasn't as if similar hierarchies did not exist within Sikhism. Upper-caste Sikhs like Jats often oppressed the Sikh Dalits. Mannu's initiation into crime was purportedly because of such an incident.

Before he became a gun-toting gangster, thirty-two-year-old Manpreet made a respectable living as a carpenter in his village. 'His forearms were amongst the strongest I have seen,' recalled a police officer. That may have been the result of his everyday work with a planer, working rhythmically to smoothen wood, but it resulted in him being known for his exceptionally strong arms.

Perhaps life would have continued in that way, had a group of powerful Jats not started harassing his younger sister. The family decided to ignore it at first, thinking it would pass. Then, one day, she returned home pale and with fear-stricken eyes. Soon, she stopped stepping out altogether. That was in August 2010.

Mannu, unable to sit quietly and ignore the harassment any longer, decided to take on the stalkers. Armed with only a stick, and accompanied by his friend Sukhraj and some others, Mannu beat the Jats who had been harassing his sister black and blue. He was arrested and booked for an attempt to murder. 'Some wild trees are only disciplined by pruning,' a police official later recalled him saying. When Mannu came out on bail a year later, he promised his mother he wouldn't indulge in violence again. And perhaps he meant it too. But the harassers of his sister and family resurfaced.

The Jats took to harassing the family on different pretexts. There were allegations that the local police also helped them. As was expected after such repeated provocation, a brawl ensued and Mannu Kusa was booked again for an attempt to murder on 11 August 2014. The Jats, meanwhile, went scot-free.

This time, Mannu Kusa had had enough. Along with Sukhraj, Mannu escaped from prison and managed to procure some weapons. The armed men returned to hunt for the Jats who had been causing them such misery. On 11 September 2014, Mannu Kusa shot Jugraj Singh, while he was ploughing his fields on his tractor, as revenge for his and his family's continuous harassment.

What Mannu did not know was that Jugraj was a close friend of gangster Sukhpreet Singh, alias Budha, who was one of the top members of the dreaded Davinder Bambiha gang.

Now, Budha's cronies started harassing Mannu's family, pressurising them to divulge his whereabouts. In quick retaliation, Mannu cornered one such crony called Gagnaa and shot at both his ankles.

This only made matters worse since Gagnaa was Sukhpreet Budha's cousin. The matter was now personal for Budha and the Davinder Bambiha gang. More than a year later, in late 2015, Moga police caught Kusa and threw him into Faridkot jail, straight into Budha's den. Budha was an undertrial in the same prison, cornered Mannu one night and had him stripped and beaten. The attackers, led by one Harjit Singh, alias Penta, video-recorded the beating, especially men whacking Mannu's head with slippers. The humiliation was symbolic.

In the Jat land, Dalits are treated like *paon ki jutti*, slippers, with no great value. Discrimination, while illegal, inhumane and unlawful as per the Constitution of India, is deeply entrenched. Mannu Kusa's family converted to Sikhism with the belief that their lot in society would improve. Sikhism views all humans as of one caste and from one seed. But the reality that they were facing now was very different.

Not only did the assailants beat up Mannu, they also circulated the video on social media as a lesson and warning for others.

Mannu's ordeal of abuse, frequent beatings and humiliation in jail continued right until Jaggu Bhagwanpuria was transferred to the same prison. Jaggu was a rival of the Bambiha gang. He took Mannu under his wing and protected him in and around the barracks, and also funded his court trial.

For Mannu, Jaggu was an angel sent by god.

When he was released on bail a year later, Mannu was no longer an oppressed victim with no recourse. He was now connected to gangster Jaggu Bhagwanpuria and through him, became linked to the Lawrence Bishnoi syndicate.

They had a common enemy—the Davinder Bambiha-Sukhpreet Budha-Lucky Patial gang.

Mannu met Jagroop Singh, also known as Roopa, through another friend of Bhagwanpuria's. Not only was Roopa a criminal, he was also a drug addict who had apparently been disowned by his family. In April 2022, the two killed Penta. It was payback time.

After the murder, Mannu and Roopa fled in a used white Corolla. Saraj Mintu, another friend and accomplice of Bhagwanpuria's, provided that car. A few weeks later, Mintu would give another Corolla to Mannu and Roopa through one Manpreet Bhau, who would be the first man arrested in the Sidhu Moosewala murder case from Dehradun.

Mannu Kusa, the man with the solid forearm muscles, had no problem firing his AK-47 assault rifle at the singer that ill-fated evening on 29 May. He jumped out of the Corolla and fired like a man possessed. He became the face of terror when the police released his poster later—a loving and dutiful son lost somewhere behind the bloodshot eyes, the eyelids permanently heavy from doses of heroin.

PRIYAVRAT FAUJI

On a hot afternoon in June 2015, the village of Garhi Sisana in Sonepat, Haryana, came alive with the beating of drums. Young and old alike made a beeline towards the village centre where a local boy called Priyavrat was being felicitated. Wrestling was the favoured sport in the village; the sport separated the vagabonds from those with purpose. To earn the respect of the villagers, one had to distinguish themselves in the field. Recruited under the Boys Sports Company Scheme of the Indian

Army, Priyavrat had done just that. The twenty-six-year-old was a champion and had made the village proud.

Not only that, Priyavrat had arrived with additional honour. Recruited as a soldier, he was promoted to subedar as a reward for winning the gold medal in the Army's inter-regiments competitions held in Pune.

He also earned a month's leave and the nickname 'Fauji'. But within a month, Priyavrat had turned into a villain for the village. He got involved in a brawl with his relatives over an old land dispute. A man called Rookhi died due to injuries suffered in the brawl. Fauji was booked for the murder along with others. The wrestler who had defeated so many in the ring lost to himself as a life of respectability slipped from his fingers. Fauji was arrested and put away in Sonepat jail where he met seasoned criminals and joined them. Out on bail, he became an associate of a gangster, Ramkaran, a distant relative, and together, they started to commit crimes. Sometime in 2020, Fauji returned home for a few days. Reports say his uncle gave him a good beating and bade him to leave the bad company he was in. Fauji never returned to his village again.

His criminal record grew and as per the police dossiers on him, Priyavrat killed Haryana gangster Ajay Barona's father on 18 March 2021. After that, he went underground and remained in hiding till he surfaced in the Moosewala murder case.

Fauji was the de facto chief of the six shooters. He was the one who was in touch with Canada-based Goldy

Brar over the internet phone. He was also talking to others and coordinating logistical support.

Fauji's way of doing things was different from that of Lawrence and Goldy. His initial plan was for the shooters to dress up as cops, gain easy access to Moosewala and shoot him, maybe even in his own house. Fauji also suggested using grenades. To escape suspicion, he planned to get a woman dressed as a lady constable to accompany them on their mission to kill Moosewala.

However, neither Lawrence Bishnoi nor Goldy Brar were in favour of his ideas. They probably did not see any heroism or gangster's swagger in Fauji's idea of carrying out the killing dressed as cops. After all, the image was as important as the actual crime. It was all about the fear the names of the assailants would attract after the deed had been done.

Fauji's lifestyle was different from that of the others. He was known to indulge in the pleasures of the flesh. He is said to have had four girlfriends, one of whom he had wanted to take along for the operation.

Little did he know that his girlfriends would prove to be his undoing.

ROOPA

According to the Punjab Opioid Dependence Survey (PODS), 2015, there were an estimated 8.6 lakh drug users in Punjab. Many of them were teenagers.[1]

Jagroop Singh of the village of Jaura in Tarn Taran district was one of them. The younger son of a farmer who owned just two acres of land, Roopa was constantly in the shadow of his elder brother, a jawan in the Indian Army and the pride of their family. Roopa started using drugs early while still in school and then sank deeper into the quicksand of narcotics. The jibes of friends and fellow villagers about the difference between the two brothers only caused him to withdraw further into himself. Taunts about him being a curse on his family led him down the road to self-destruction. From stealing money, jewellery and even utensils from his house to buy drugs, Roopa progressed to became a drug peddler.

The equation was simple. Roopa would keep 10 per cent of the drugs for himself and sell the rest at a premium to desperate addicts. He didn't stop there and took every opportunity to strengthen his position within the world of crime. He was a notorious snatcher, drug smuggler and finally, a sharpshooter.

His dealings with drugs and hardened criminals meant his life was hurtling towards imminent doom. His association with Bhagwanpuria, and later with Mannu Kusa, may have been the reason he was in the car that day, shooting Sidhu Moosewala, but his life story had already been following a trajectory which was similar to that of many drug addicts in Punjab. From the land of bravehearts and warriors to the land of drug menace, Punjab's reputation has seen a marked shift. Young lives in Punjab have been drawn into the tight grip of drug abuse, leading to a life of crime, and eventually dying an untimely death.

At any given time in Punjab in the last decade, more than 50 per cent of the inmates in the twenty-nine big and small jails were drug addicts-cum-peddlers or smugglers.[2] Punjab topped the country in the number of cases registered under the Narcotic Drugs and Psychotropic Substances (NDPS) Act, 1985, from 2016 to 2019.

'He was dead to us the day he became a drug addict,' Roopa's mother Palwinder would say later. 'He sold household things. He looted from others too. But was it just our fault? No. The government is responsible for the tragic end Roopa and other youths like him meet with.'

ANKIT SERSA

If you were to look at Ankit Sersa's face in the photograph that went viral after Sidhu Moosewala's killing, it would most likely evoke a feeling of pity rather than fear or disgust. A fresh-faced youth with hardly a trace of a beard on his cheeks, Sersa looks even younger than his nineteen years. His eyes are lit up with mischief, typical of teenagers, high on life and youth.

But when you look beyond his face, your heart may freeze. Ankit is seen squatting on the floor next to dozens of bullets arranged in the name of Moosewala. He brandishes 9mm pistols in both his hands.

The pistols were not just props for the picture. Ankit had a rare talent—he could shoot with both hands and that too, simultaneously. The ambidextrous teenage gangster was one of a kind in the Delhi and Punjab Police records, at least had been in the last few decades. It was he who ran out of the car shooting at Moosewala with pistols held in both hands.[3]

How did Sersa, so young that he just about made it across the threshold of adolescence, end up at the shoot-out? It was perhaps because of his penchant for a life that was out of his reach. As per police records, Ankit Sersa had a weakness—a deep hunger for name, fame and a high-flying lifestyle. And then there was his role model: Lawrence Bishnoi.

Youngest of six siblings, including four sisters, Ankit was the darling of his family. His lower-middle-class parents in the village of Sersa tried to fulfil as many of his demands as they could. Thoroughly pampered by his family, with his every wish and demand met, Ankit was not used to anyone checking his behaviour. Neither his parents nor his siblings scolded him when he failed several times and dropped out of school in class 10. Even when he stole a mobile phone from a relative's house, it was overlooked as something trivial. No one disciplined him when they should have.

In the middle of all this, the COVID-19 pandemic struck India and a severe lockdown was imposed. Sersa's parents lost their jobs when the factory they worked at retrenched several employees. Ankit is said to have tried to find a job but could not. He started to spend more time with wastrels and petty criminals and soon heard of Lawrence Bishnoi, who was spoken of amongst his friends in tones of veneration. Impressed by what he was hearing, Ankit decided he wanted to work with Lawrence. In fact, he wanted to *be* Lawrence. To his young and impressionable mind, Lawrence and his infamy seemed impossibly glamorous. He too wanted a huge social media following. He wanted to strike fear and awe in the hearts and minds of people like Lawrence did. He wanted people to talk about him the way they spoke of Lawrence.

The teenage shooter went the closest to Moosewala to shoot him, according to police files. Sersa's name will forever be linked to the Moosewala shooting. After all, some of his disastrous ambitions did come true.

DEEPAK MUNDI AND KASHISH

'Only I will kill Moosewala, no one else,' thundered Deepak Mundi. The shooters had all assembled in one of their hideouts in the village of Ramditte Wala, about 5.2 km northeast of the village of Moosa, five days before the murder.

But Mundi turned out to be the last to shoot at the singer. He also turned out to be the smartest. He was caught 105 days after the killing—a record of sorts. By then, he was the only one on the run.[4] On 19 June, a day before Fauji and Kashish were caught from Kutch in Gujarat, he got separated from them.

The day before Ankit Sersa and his accomplice, Sachin Bhiwani, were caught near the Inter-State Bus Terminal in New Delhi, Mundi got separated from them too.

Despite being regularly admonished by Fauji, he rarely covered his face in public. 'He left us and went his way,' Fauji told the police.

Mundi is also said to have been in touch with the Corolla module of the shooters—Roopa and Mannu Kusa—before the Punjab Police killed them in an encounter on 20 July in the village of Bhakna in Tarn Taran, not far from the international border with Pakistan. The police had given code names to the two groups of shooters, who had come in two different vehicles. The Bolero module, had four—Fauji, Ankit, Deepak Mundi and Kashish. The second, called the Corolla module, had two shooters—Roopa and Mannu Kusa.

To nab Mundi, the Punjab and Delhi police teams had to join forces—another rarity. His closest friend in the group was Kashish.

Kashish, about twenty-four, belonged to Beri town in Jhajjar, Haryana. From a poor family, he could not continue his studies after class 10, learning to drive instead. He drove a taxi and even a truck before he got involved in a brawl in Beri, in 2021. Kashish was sent to jail, where he came in contact with different gangsters. He also caught the attention of Goldy Brar's men, especially for his driving skills. When a CCTV grab of the shooters at a petrol pump was released to the public, Kashish was spotted in the driver's seat.

On 10 September, Deepak Mundi was arrested near Pani Tanki, not too far from the Indo-Nepal Border in Siliguri, West Bengal. The police said the place was a transit route to Nepal. The land-locked country nestled almost in the centre of the great Himalayas between India and China is considered to be a haven for criminals escaping from India. Once they enter Nepal, they are out of the reach of Indian police. They can use fake documents to fly to other countries. Mundi was caught before he entered Nepal. Whether or not he had any links with the Naxals could not be established.

It was discovered that the six-shooters received only Rs 4.5 lakh in total for the murder. They were given Rs 2.5 lakh as an advance and 2 lakh after the shooting. They, thus, appear to have killed a young man, whose net worth at the time of his death was around 112 crore, just for seventy-five thousand rupees per head. The others who provided logistical support or carried out recces were given a maximum of ten thousand rupees. 'Some were promised prominence in the gangs, money for a vehicle, house or their sisters' weddings,' revealed a police official.

The youngest shooter, Ankit Sersa, claimed Lawrence and Goldy Brar had promised them one crore for the job but they never received that money. They were told that their names would become so big that they could later earn crores of rupees simply on the strength of the terror they invoked. That was not to be.

SEVEN

CHAUHAN

When the Senior Superintendent of Police (SSP) of Mansa, Gaurav Toora, learnt about the attack on Sidhu Moosewala, he immediately set about informing his superiors, right up to the Director General of Police, V.K. Bhawra. But one of the first calls he made was to Assistant Inspector General (AIG) of Police G.S. Chauhan. Chauhan was the liaison officer for the Punjab Police's Anti-Gangster Task Force (AGTF), and within the force, he was known as an encyclopaedia on the gangsters of Punjab. Who killed whom? Who belonged to which gang? What did they deal in? With whom did a particular gangster's loyalty lie? Chauhan had all the information at his fingertips. In his late fifties, Chauhan's painter's brush moustache and crown of silver hair set him apart, as did his alacrity and experience. He was the axle around which spun the Punjab Police's wheel of justice against gangsters.

When the call came, Chauhan was in his study. 'Damn!' he said when SSP Toora informed him about the attack on Moosewala. 'Has he survived?' he asked, as he hunted for the television remote. The TV came alive with visuals of the crime spot in the village of Jawaharke, on the first news channel he came across. 'Taken to the hospital. He is hit. Badly hit. Many shots were fired. A lot many.' Toora said, his voice grave.

⎯⎯⎯⎯

Chauhan's mind raced as he disconnected the call. He had been about to settle down with a peg of Scotch and plan the week ahead. Now he knew all plans would have to be cast aside. This was going to blow up and the police had best be prepared. He busied himself calling his superiors, his team and the field units.

'Get cracking immediately,' said Promod Ban, Additional Director General of Police (ADGP) and head of the AGTF. Tall and dashing, Ban had taken charge of the newly-formed AGTF barely a month ago. A senior IPS officer, his bright eyes spoke of his intelligence. Ban wasn't one to sit in his room, weave theories and give orders. He was known to be action-oriented—be it gunning down gangsters, smugglers and kidnappers, or countering terrorists.

Before the AGTF was formed in April that year, it was the OCCU that investigated gangsters and kept them in check.[1] It was the OCCU which had recommended a security cover for Moosewala. The AGTF came into being when Bhagwant Mann of the AAP became the chief minister of Punjab on 16 March 2022. Soon after coming to power, he directed Police Chief V.K. Bhawra to set up the special task force. Mann's intention was simple. He wanted to send across a strong message that his government would crack down on the gangsters running amok in Punjab, many of whom openly enjoyed the patronage of the AAP'S political rivals—mainly the Congress and the SAD. In actuality, aside from the new nomenclature, AGTF was simply OCCU—but with a severe defect. The OCCU had integrated units of field and intelligence teams that worked together. The AGTF, it was decided, would be purely operation-based. While the field team remained under the AGTF, the intelligence unit was moved to the Counter Intelligence and Internal Security units of the Punjab police.

Under the OCCU, information from field and intelligence reached one unit, one officer, making it much more comprehensive. But now, the teams were separated and worked under different heads. The plan was to have meetings once or twice a month to share, discuss and plot the course of action ahead. After Moosewala was gunned down, many officers connected with the case privately confessed that they had sent several alerts to their seniors to strengthen the singer's security. Instead, his security was pruned. Could the killing have been prevented if there had been greater cohesiveness in the teams or one chain of command? This embarrassing question has plagued the Punjab Police since the day of the killing. Unfortunately, there are no clear answers.

Eventually, forty-five days after the shoot-out, the first head rolled when DGP V.K. Bhawra was removed from his post. Gaurav Yadav was posted as the new DGP of the Punjab Police.

After speaking to ADGP Ban, Chauhan called his most trusted and capable colleague, Deputy Superintendent of Police (DSP) Bikramjit Brar. A highly decorated officer, Brar was known for his work against gangsters and terrorists. He was a recipient of the President's Police Medal for gallantry with a double bar. It meant he was among the few officers who had received the award three times in a row for different operations against gangsters.

After a quick chat with Brar, Chauhan hurriedly picked up his pistol and the diaries that contained his notes and rushed out. He had briefed Brar about the shoot-out and asked him to activate his sources. Chauhan also activated the technical team, the cyber wing of the Punjab Police to check active mobile phones near the crime spot.

Moosewala's killing was a sensational event. The newly-formed AAP government would expect quick results. Chauhan was aware of the challenge. The gang wars that the AGTF, and earlier the OCCU, had been trying to curb were growing out of hand. The gangs were becoming bigger and more audacious, and each killing was turning out to be bloodier than the one before. Chauhan knew that Moosewala's murder would draw the country's attention to Punjab, but it was not a standalone case. It was the latest in a series of brutal killings that Chauhan had been tracking for quite some time. All the murders were fresh in his mind. The menace of the gangsters had been one of the main issues during the Punjab Assembly elections in February. The new government had just announced the setting up of the AGTF and it was yet to have district units.

The AGTF had its headquarters at Mohali, where it operated from the third floor of the Punjab Police Intelligence Headquarters, with other units operating from different bases. The top cops of the unit, like Chauhan and Brar, operated out of the Mohali office. Mohali is situated close to Chandigarh on the eastern end of Punjab. For speedy operations, the government planned to set up smaller units of field operatives in various districts. But the AGTF had, as of now, only one field unit in the state of Punjab. Luckily, it was stationed in Bathinda, about 62 km away, just an hour's drive from where Moosewala was killed. By the time Chauhan and Brar reached the crime spot from Mohali, in about three hours, the field unit, working on their instructions, had secured the crime spot.

THE GANGS AND GANG WARS OF PUNJAB

According to the Punjab Police records of 2018, there were about 550 gangsters, belonging to fifty-seven gangs, operating in Punjab. In July 2022, that number had grown to about 1,200 members belonging to seventy gangs. The state had fallen prey to the gang menace, with each gang exerting influence on a specific area of the state. Punjab is divided culturally and geographically into three regions with rivers forming the boundaries. The Majha region comprises the area between the Ravi and Beas rivers. The Doaba region is between the Beas and Sutlej rivers. And the Malwa region lies below the Sutlej, broadly between Sutlej and Ghaggar. It extends up to the shared borders with Haryana, Rajasthan and Himachal Pradesh.

In the latest dossier updated on 31 October 2022, the AGTF identified ten groups as the 'parent gangs' or 'gangster groups' active in the state. There were 293 confirmed members of these gangster groups. Amongst them, 160 were behind bars or had been 'eliminated' in police encounters, or in gang wars.

About sixty other gangs were associated with one or more parent gang. There were splinter groups as well. The number of gang members was anywhere between 1,200 and 2,000. These included women, who arranged hideouts and kept the supply chain alive.

The dossier draws a detailed map of the gangs' activities, members, links and rivalries with each other. To quote directly from it: 'These gangs are indulging in organised crimes like contract killing/attempt to murder, shoot-outs, gang wars, murder in police custody/jail custody, attack on police personnel, kidnapping for ransom, extortion, running protection money rackets, armed protection to illegal activity, gun running, highway robberies, bank dacoities, cash van looting, snatching of vehicles, snatching of money, etc. A review of the criminal gangs that are active in Punjab was carried out. The profile of gangster groups, based on interrogation of various criminals and information received from various sources, has been updated.

- New alignments among different gangster groups have come to the fore.
- New hideouts have been identified.
- Several associates of gangsters hitherto unknown were also identified.
- At present, ten gangster groups are active in Punjab.'

As per the dossier, the ten groups were:

1. **The Jaipal Group:** The son of a cop, Jaipal Bhullar of Ferozepur was a national-level hammer throw athlete, before a dispute over selection in a team turned into a brawl and led to a police case against him in Ludhiana in 2003–04. Bhullar ended up in jail where he was in the company of dreaded criminals who treated him as a hero due to his fearless nature and muscular body. After coming in contact with anti-social elements in jail, Bhullar took their help to kidnap the son of a cinema hall owner in Ludhiana, in 2004. He gained much notoriety for the case, and

his sporting career came to a definite end. Later, he got in touch with another gangster called Shera Khuban, and then met Jaswinder Singh, alias Rocky. In 2010, Rocky was considered the most dangerous gangster in Punjab, and was an influential figure. He patronised several gangsters and, according to sources in the police, he nurtured Bhullar, making the latter more powerful. However, when Rocky turned politician and joined the SAD, he worked on improving his image. It is alleged that police eliminated some gangsters, including Bhullar's friend Shera Khuban, in Bathinda in September 2012, as Rocky was inimical towards him. Infuriated by the turn of events, Bhullar formed his own gang and declared revenge. In April 2016, his promise of revenge was fulfilled when he killed Rocky in Parwanoo, Himachal Pradesh. Several gangs apart from Bhullar's celebrated Rocky's murder, creating posts on Facebook which alleged that Rocky had been a snitch.

In June 2021, West Bengal Police, on 'live information' from the Punjab Police, killed Bhullar and two others in an encounter in Kolkata. Bhullar may be dead but his gang lives on. His brother, Amritpal Bhullar, and a close aide, Gagan Judge, are reportedly running the gang from jail. Arsh Dala from Canada and Gurjant, alias Janta, from Australia, are active members of this gang. The gang is active in parts of Malwa, Haryana and Chandigarh and is known for its involvement in murder, extortion and terrorist activities.

2. **The Jaggu Bhagwanpuria Gang (earlier Sukha Khalwan Gang):** Thirty-two-year-old Jagdeep Singh, alias Jaggu Bhagwanpuria of Surat Malhi, Batala, is the head of this gang. He is presently in Tihar Jail, New Delhi. Both the Congress and the SAD have allegedly had links with him at different times. He is close to the Lawrence Bishnoi group and is said to have supplied shooters—Roopa and Mannu Kusa—for Moosewala's killing. He is influential in the Majha region of Punjab, especially Amritsar, Tarn Taran, Gurdaspur and Ferozepur. A former kabaddi player, he organises supari killings and kabaddi leagues, due to which he is in direct conflict with other gangsters interested in these leagues.

3. **The Lawrence Bishnoi Group:** Run by thirty-year-old Lawrence Bishnoi, the gang is considered the biggest and most influential in Punjab. Bishnoi also heads syndicates in Punjab, Haryana, Rajasthan and the NCR. He is said to be controlling extortion racquets all over Punjab and the NCR, and has links with gangsters abroad.

    The Jaipal group, the Bhagwanpuria gang and the Lawrence Bishnoi group are friendly with each other.

4. **Rinda Group:** Started by Harwinder Singh Sandhu, the Rinda group operates from Pakistan and is pro-Khalistan. Thirty-five-year-old Sandhu, alias Rinda,

is from Nanded, and was a gangster before turning terrorist. He is involved in terror activities and uses the network of other gangs in Punjab to carry out anti-India and pro-Khalistan attacks. Almost all the gangs of Punjab have worked with, or for, him at some time. Rinda is dangerous as he has the network to supply weapons, drugs, fake currency and trained shooters. There are rumours that he has died, though this has not been confirmed by the police.

5. **Dilpreet Singh, alias Baba of Noorpur Bedi** is the head of this group active in Punjab and Haryana, especially Chandigarh. Its area of influence is the Doaba region. The group has been involved in extortion threats to Punjabi singers and actors. In 2018, they attacked Punjabi singer Parmish Verma. Dilpreet Singh is currently in jail but his group is in alliance with gangster groups of Rinda, Davinder Bambiha, Gurpreet Sekhon and Sukhpreet Singh, alias Budha.

6. **Bambiha Group:** Slim and athletic, Davinder Singh Sidhu, alias Bambiha, was another kabaddi player who turned gangster. Originally from village of Bambiha, he got involved in the world of crime in 2010 when a college brawl in the eighteenth year of his life in Moga led to him being booked for murder along with a friend. He formed his gang soon after and started influencing kabaddi matches. Bambiha was killed in an encounter in Bathinda in September 2016. After him, Harsimran Singh, alias Simma, from

Faridkot, became the head of the gang. Lucky Patial is the leading operative of the Bambiha gang, and carries out operations from a jail in Armenia. Another key organiser of the group is Budha. This group is close to the Dilpreet Baba group.

7. **Harry Chatha Group:** Supreet Singh, alias Harry Chatha, of Batala, is the head of this group. The operations of the gang are run from somewhere in Europe with the help of Inter-Services Intelligence (ISI) of Pakistan. The Harry Chatha Group is in an alliance with gangster groups led by Gurpreet Sekhon and Davinder Bambiha and in opposition to gangster groups led by Jaipal and Jaggu Bhagwanpuria. The group has its roots in the Majha region, but is active in the tri-city (Chandigarh, Mohali and Panchkula) region. Harry Chatha is a person of interest in several cases.

8. **Sekhon Group:** Headed by Gurpreet Singh Sekhon, this group is in alliance with the Harry Chatha and Davinder Bambiha gangs and thus in opposition to the Lawrence Bishnoi, Jaipal and Jaggu Bhagwanpuria gangs. Ramanjeet Singh, alias Romi, currently in a Hong Kong jail, is the manager of this group. The Sekhon group is in touch with Sikh hardliners and with Pakistan's ISI through Ramanjeet Singh and Aman Pannu (also in a Hong Kong jail). This group has its roots in the Malwa region.

9. **Sukhpreet Budha:** Though running the affairs of the Bambiha group in line with Lucky Patial, Budha has

his own gang as well, which works in tandem with the Bambiha group and its associates.

10. **Aman Jaito group:** The tenth group is of Aman Jaito, who also works with the Bambiha group while strengthening his own gang.

What is worth noting is the fact that Jaipal, Bhagwanpuria and Lawrence are directly opposed to the Bambiha, Chatha and Sekhon gangs. In fact, the latter three are more in sync with Pakistan-based anti-India agencies, drugs smugglers and Sikh hardliners. The gangster Tirath Singh from the Jaipal group has friendly ties with Gurpreet Singh Sekhon's group. The two have worked together on some crimes.

The Rinda gang as well as the Dilpreet Baba gang have good relations with almost all the other groups.

THE GANG WARS

Chandigarh's Sector 26 is the place to be if one wants to experience high-octane nightlife. It is popular with youngsters from the tri-city area, as well as the neighbouring regions of Haryana and Himachal.

The nightclubs and discos pulsate with people out for a good time, fuelled by adrenaline and substances. Alcohol and drugs are common. The police know that the combination of youth, free-flowing liquor and easily accessible drugs is a recipe for disaster, but the presence of a khaki uniform at a place where people have gathered to have a good time is bad for business. To maintain a semblance of order, the nightclub owners have their own breed of enforcers—bouncers. Controlling a crowd that is high on drugs and alcohol is not easy. Most of the time, a bouncer's job is to cool down the easily inflammable tempers of young people, particularly those more intoxicated than the others. But there are times when the bouncers clash with other bouncers or well-built youths from the hinterlands of Punjab or the Jat land of Haryana. It could be over a perceived slight or just a general disregard for authority. In such circumstances, the situation can often turn ugly. In 2016, Sector 26 witnessed several such clashes over crowd management.

In one instance, bouncers Amit, alias Meet, and Akhil were trying to control an unruly group of people from Haryana at a nightclub. The argument turned ugly. The youths had a friend called Gagan, a bouncer at another club who was also the son of a Punjab Police Assistant sub-inspector. They summoned him there to add weight to their side. But on that day, Amit and Akhil prevailed over Gagan and the others.

Now, Meet was influential in the business. He had connections and even supplied bouncers to twelve clubs in the city. One of the bouncers he knew was Lucky Patial, who would go on to run the Davinder Bambiha gang. It was well-known in the area that attacking Meet was not a good idea. But a few days after this incident, Gagan, along with some accomplices, opened fire at Meet and Akhil while they were exercising in a gym.

Akhil was wounded. Meet escaped. A case of attempt to murder was registered. Lucky Patial and others entered the scene, and a compromise was decided on. The terms were that Gagan would apologise in public and a truce would follow. But Meet was not content with a mere apology. He wanted to humiliate Gagan. He insisted that Gagan's father, a cop, apologise by bowing before Meet and placing his turban at his feet. This was asking for too much. But Gagan's father, who wanted to protect his son at all costs, did as he was told and apologised. He hoped the matter would now be resolved and peace would return.

It did not.

Meet did not honour his word and refused to give a statement to the police that would exonerate Gagan. This was crossing a line, as far as Gagan was concerned.

On 9 May 2017, Gagan, along with four shooters, killed Meet outside a temple in Saketri, a village located at the meeting point of three cities—Mohali, Chandigarh and Panchkula. Meet died in front of his mother, who had accompanied him to the temple.

Lucky Patial, who had already started his foray into the world of crime, was livid when he heard of Meet's murder. However, he also learnt that Gagan was close to Lawrence Bishnoi, his arch-rival. They were already engaged in a turf war over a larger share of extortion money from the area. Meanwhile, another altercation occurred in Faridkot town, some 250 km away from Chandigarh. Gurlal Brar, a cousin of gangster Goldy

Brar (the main conspirator in the Moosewala killing) and close aide of Lawrence Bishnoi, had an altercation with one Beant Brar, who was a part of the Bambiha-Patial group. Gurlal reportedly fired at Beant in the latter's house and wounded him. Gurlal and Beant were both vying to establish their dominance in the liquor and gambling business in the region. Matters kept worsening between the two gangs. Another member of the Bambiha group, Lavi Deora, was killed at a festival in Faridkot by members of the Lawrence Bishnoi gang a few days later.

Police believe that some 'saner' voices within these gangs tried to play mediator, including student-leader-turned-politician Vicky Middukhera. Because of the intervention, immediate follow-up killings stopped. It is not uncommon for calmer voices to mediate in such gang wars, as prolonged violence and carnage not only disturbs the peace amongst them but is also bad for business.

There was a slight lull in the bloodshed, but Beant Brar of the Bambiha-Patial group was still smarting after being shot at by Gurlal. He was lying low, waiting for just the right opportunity to exact revenge. He found his allies in two daredevil youths of Jaito, Faridkot: Neeraj, alias Chaska, and Mandeep Mann, alias Mandy. They indulged in snatching and robberies but wanted to do something bigger. So, Beant tasked them with killing Gurlal Brar.[2]

The two spent some days on a recce of Chandigarh clubs. They rode around on a bike, trailing Gurlal at a distance and got a sense of his movements. On

10 October 2020, Beant asked them to choose a day, steal a car, kill Gurlal and flee. The two were trying to locate a vehicle, specifically a Toyota Fortuner, which they could steal for use in the crime. Much to their surprise, they found Gurlal Brar getting into a Fortuner right before their eyes, completely out of sync with his normal routine. 'Kill him now,' Beant Brar reportedly ordered the two over the phone when they informed him.

The two shot Brar right there and fled the scene. Police later found their bike abandoned only a kilometre away. It had developed a snag. The shooters had forced out the passengers of another car and made their getaway. Police arrested a drug addict called Smackiya for helping the shooters, but they could not nab either Chaska or Mandy.

It is alleged that Gurlal Brar had stakes in a music label called Thug Life. He had wanted singer Sidhu Moosewala to release songs only with his label. Gurlal's murder angered Goldy Brar and Lawrence Bishnoi. In a YouTube interview after Moosewala's death, Goldy Brar can be heard telling journalist Ritesh Lakhi: 'Gurlal's murder was an attack on our family. That is not done. They will have to pay.'[3]

To avenge Gurlal's killing, Bishnoi's men killed his namesake, Gurlal Pehalwan, on 18 February 2021.[4] A politician close to Lucky Patial and the Bambiha gang, Pehalwan was the district Youth Congress president. He was shot thirteen times and took five bullets in the abdomen and two in the chest. The last two shots were fired into the back of his head as the body lay face down on the road.

The shoot-outs were getting more frequent and the murders more and more common. In July 2021, Kulbir Naruana, a gangster-turned-social-worker, was killed by his former aide Mandeep, alias Manna, who had switched to the Bambiha gang. Naruana is said to have been close to Lawrence Bishnoi once, but took to social work with a view to later join politics.

Goldy Brar, who wanted to wipe out the Bambiha-Patial gang to avenge the killing of his cousin Gurlal Brar, targeted and killed gangster Rana Kandowalia in Amritsar on 4 August 2021 outside KD hospital.

Kandowalia was also an enemy of Jaggu Bhagwanpuria, which worked out well for Bishnoi. Lawrence and Bhagwanpuria had a reciprocal relationship. They worked independently but helped each other when necessary.

The gang wars had escalated dangerously. Four days after the death of Kandowalia, Vicky Middukhera, who was known to be very close to Bishnoi, was attacked. Middukhera had a promising political career ahead of him. He allegedly handled the finances of the Bishnoi gang and also mediated disputes between different criminal groups. As far as gangsters went, he was well liked and respected. On 7 August 2021, fifteen shots were fired at him in broad daylight, in Mohali.[5] The Lucky Patial gang had, with the help of the Kaushal gang, sent four men from Haryana to carry out the task. The murder was to avenge the killings of Gurlal Pehalwan and Rana Kandowalia murders. With the death of Middukhera, it was as if war had been declared.

On 14 March 2022, four men from the Kaushal-Daggar-Bambiha gang walked into a kabaddi match in Nakodar, Jalandhar. They challenged the chief organiser and famous kabaddi player Sandeep Nangal Ambian, and shot him at point-blank range.

Ambian was shot in the centre of his forehead. The kabaddi league he was running belonged to Jaggu Bhagwanpuria.

Lawrence and Bhagwanpuria had had enough. They joined hands to hit the most high-profile of targets—Sidhu Moosewala.

⸻

G.S Chauhan went over his notes about the gang wars with DSP Brar, as they made their way to the scene of crime in the village of Jawaharke.

He made another note: Panjab University, Chandigarh!

Lawrence was, after all, not the only one who emerged out of the student politics of the university as a gangster. The bitterly contested student elections held annually in the 140-year-old educational institution had produced individuals who rise to power with the help of rowdyism, threats and power stemming from money and weapons.

There was Prabhjinder Singh, famous as Dimpy Chandbhan, was the first gangster in post-terrorism Punjab belonging to the village of Chandbhan in Faridkot. Police officials call him the godfather of gangsters, responsible for different gangs in Punjab. His clout became apparent towards the end of terrorism in Punjab in mid-1996 when he killed Makhan Singh, a student leader at Panjab University. Chandbhan patronised many other youth leaders, and his influence remained till July 2006. It was alleged that he was killed by his former protégé Jaswinder Singh, alias Rocky. Rocky was acquitted in 2014 of the charges.[6] By that time, he had become another Chandbhan. He also patronised gangsters and student leaders besides wining and dining politicians. He was linked to the SAD and later unsuccessfully contested elections.

In the course of his shift from gangster to politician, Rocky was accused by some gangsters of snitching on them. One of them, named Jaipal, killed Rocky in Parwanoo, a border town in Himachal Pradesh adjoining Haryana and Punjab, in 2016. Jaipal and Shera Khuban, who died in a police encounter, were both associated with Panjab University student politics.

The Panjab University, where former prime minister Dr Manmohan Singh used to teach between 1957 and 1966, is plagued by bad press in the present day because of the thugs who swarm its grounds. With the death of Moosewala, public attention refocused on the 140-year-old institution and the rise of the gang culture that it had fostered.

While G.S. Chauhan meticulously pored over his notes in a bid to catch Moosewala's killers, someone sitting nearly 300 km away was also mulling over how to draw the net tighter around the lot.

EIGHT

THE CATCHER

Hargobinder Singh Dhaliwal—fondly called Harry by his colleagues—was enjoying a rare peaceful Sunday at home. An IPS officer of the 1997 batch, Dhaliwal headed the Special Cell (SC) of the Delhi Police, which has a wide jurisdiction. With its mandate to spot and break any emerging network of gangsters to prevent even a ripple of violence reaching Delhi, the SC had a tough job, as did Dhaliwal.

Broad-shouldered, athletic and clean-shaven, Dhaliwal looked unlike a typical Punjabi Jat police officer. His sharp features lent his face a certain resolve. To set it off, his eyes had a hard glint, earned from arresting many top-notch criminals and interrogating hardened gangsters. There seemed to always be the hint of a smile on his lips, especially when dealing with tricky questions from journalists. The Special Commissioner of Police knew his job—and he knew it well.

Dhaliwal was an alumnus of Panjab University. While studying for his postgraduate degree in Management and then English literature, he had observed first-hand the rise of Dimpy Chandbhan, the first gangster to emerge in post-terrorism Punjab. Today, the university is notorious for being a breeding ground for gangsters. Perhaps it is poetic justice that the officer in charge of busting these gangs is also from the same university. Not only that, Dhaliwal's ancestors were from a village in Moga, in the Malwa region of Punjab. Most of the gangsters in modern Punjab—Bishnoi, Goldy Brar, Gurpreet Sekhon—belong to the Malwa region. Dhaliwal understood the region, its caste matrix and its despondence well. He knew why young men, bereft of opportunities, were turning to crime to prove themselves. His understanding of the language and the culture was a definite advantage when trying to get into the minds of dreaded criminals.

On that fateful evening of 29 May, he had just settled down with a book when he heard his phone beeping alerts.

'Moosewala shot', the first message read. 'Dead,' another message followed.

'It's brazen ...' Dhaliwal muttered, as he scrolled through his phone. A contact had sent him a video of the incident. The video showed Moosewala's bullet-ridden body being taken out of the Thar. There was chaos everywhere.

Dhaliwal felt a pang for the young singer whose life had been cruelly cut short by the senseless gang war. He made calls to the heads of the six ranges of the SC and instructed them to put members of the SC on the case. 'This is one of the most brazen attacks on any celebrity in recent times in India. Clearly, an assault rifle has been used. This could happen anytime in the national capital where such diverse VVIPs and celebrities roam around,' he remembers telling them.

The next step was to open his laptop and review the profiles and photos of members of the gangs of Punjab and North India. There was not a moment to lose. Dhaliwal began issuing directions almost right away.

He ordered a team to get all the call detail records (CDR), tower dump (TD) and internet protocol detail records (IPDR) from Mansa. He asked them to find the active mobile phones in the region and expand the search to other towers to trace and track any unusual activity. Dhaliwal wouldn't have been surprised if the shooters chose Delhi as their hiding place. It would be so easy to disappear amidst the 15 crore-plus population of the NCR.

The TD had picked up hundreds of mobile phone calls at the time of the shoot-out. The team working on it narrowed it down to phones active near the crime spot and Moosewala's house.

The police use specialised software to analyse the data from the TD and zero in on numbers that display any suspicious activity. The CDR of these suspicious numbers are then collated and analysed. This allows them to track the movement of a suspect's mobile number. Cops also look at the duration of the calls. For example, if a call was for 15 seconds, the police would examine other calls of a similar duration from nearby towers. This way, they narrow down the search to a few suspicious numbers.

Bear in mind this entire process takes hours of sitting in front of a computer or analysing reams of paper with call records. And worse, it is a race against time. The suspect could continually be on the move and may discard the phone and use a new one. Till they are nabbed, they remain a threat to public life and property.

Criminals also keep themselves updated on the latest technological tools that the police use to track them. Most of the time, they make calls through apps like Signal, Telegram and WhatsApp, which makes it harder to track them.

'It is like searching for a mouse in a jungle,' quipped Dhaliwal. 'The gangsters do not directly talk to each other. There is no call between, say, A and B. Instead, A will call a third person C, who will put the call on speaker mode. And with another phone, he will dial B and put that call also on speaker. The conversation would be between A and B through the speakerphone. And police may not flag the calls between A and C or B and C as suspicious. Even if they do, the location and identity of the main suspect, A, would remain hidden. This is always a tough nut to crack. There are so many permutations and combinations. It is the Matrix playing in fast mode, you know?'

Another team of the SC was told to profile, trace and update the information on members of the Lawrence Bishnoi gang, the Bhagwanpuria gang, the Kaushal gang, the Bambiha gang, the Kala Jatheri gang and several others.

Then, one specific team was activated on the ground using human intelligence. Within only a few hours of Sidhu Moosewala's death, Dhaliwal and the SC were hot on the heels of the murderers. But the chase was not an easy one.

The biggest challenge for them, as Dhaliwal would tell the media later, was that they could not visit the scene of the crime. They were part of the Delhi Police and the crime scene fell under the jurisdiction of the Punjab Police. Right after a crime is committed, the area is teeming with clues—the kind of weapons used in the incident, the number of individuals involved, the vehicle used for the getaway—and it is vital for the investigating team to look for these clues before the scene gets contaminated. Only by being present at the scene can the investigators look for the minutest details that may add up. However, if Dhaliwal's SC had visited the spot, it would have led to conflict with the state police. No police team likes interference in their work and territory. Dhaliwal had to be mindful of maintaining protocol and not upsetting his counterparts in the Punjab Police. So, they kept their distance. 'It was like operating on a body from a far-off location, where we could not touch it,' Dhaliwal would later say.

As per the federal structure of India, each state or union territory (UT) has its own independent policing unit. While defence and para-military forces guard the borders of the country, the state police is responsible for law and order. Only a state police force has jurisdiction over the state. For any operation that the police of a different state may want to conduct, the jurisdiction has to be respected. Dhaliwal was making sure he did not step on any toes and jeopardise his own investigation.

Then there was the matter of Lawrence Bishnoi. Goldy Brar, a close aide of Bishnoi, had leapt forth and claimed responsibility for the killing of Moosewala. Lawrence was imprisoned in Tihar Jail in New Delhi. Dhaliwal wanted to get to him before any other agency did. Without wasting any time, just a day after the murder, the SC brought Bishnoi on a production warrant to the Rohini police station.

Dhaliwal left for the Rohini police station around midnight to have a 'chat' with Bishnoi.

As his car sped towards the police station, he checked his file for notes on Bishnoi. He spotted details of a particular operation, a unique crackdown on the gangsters that his team had carried out just two months earlier. It described the gangs and their offshoots in North India and offered a short overview of their rivalries and the history of bloodshed.

In early April of 2022, the SC of Delhi Police launched '3-P' to neutralise gangsters in North India who were eyeing the NCR for their activities. Not only were gangs killing each other's members, members of powerful syndicates operating in Punjab, Haryana, Delhi NCR and Uttar Pradesh were constantly at each other's throats.

In many ways, the network of each syndicate was quite organised. The shooters would always find a vehicle waiting for them at the next turn if they had to abandon their existing vehicle and make a quick getaway anywhere in the country. In addition, they had access to hideouts, money and the best weapons and phones, including international sim cards.

One syndicate that had emerged included Lawrence Bishnoi, Sandeep 'Kala Jathedi', Virender Pratap 'Kala Rana' and Sube Gurjar.[1] The other had Lucky Patial, Bambiha, the Kaushal Chaudhary gang, Sunil Balyan 'Tillu Tajpuriya' of the NCR, and the Neeraj Sehrawat 'Bawaniya' gang of Haryana and Noida.

The formation of syndicates aided crimes such as the murder of kabaddi player Sandeep Nangal Ambian in broad daylight and in full view of hundreds of spectators during a kabaddi match in the village of Mallian. Five unidentified assailants shot Ambian. The men apparently belonged to the Kaushal-Dagar-Bambiha gang, who had monetary interests in the game. Shot in the forehead, Ambian died, while the shooters casually strolled away from the crime scene.

Ambian's kabaddi league was said to have been 'blessed' by Jaggu Bhagwanpuria, a close friend and part of the Lawrence Bishnoi crime syndicate. According to Dhaliwal, Ambian's murder strengthened his belief that the criminal alliance needed to be profiled, mapped, identified and brought to book before they could strike again. He wanted to keep such incidents and anti-social elements far from Delhi.[2]

In November 2021, the SC first took on the Lawrence syndicate, which was active in and around New Delhi. They arrested Kala Jathedi, Kala Rana and several other members under the stringent MCOCA Act. Lawrence, too, was detained under the Act. Next, in February 2022, the Patial-Bambiha-Kaushal syndicate, which was already involved in a turf war with Lawrence and others in Haryana, Rajasthan, Punjab and Chandigarh, came under fire. The alliance had carried out the sensational Rohini courtroom murder of Jitendra Gogi, an arch-rival of Tillu Tajpuriya. Gogi had been shot eighteen times.[3]

'We conducted a long-drawn-out complex operation where massive data was requisitioned and analysed on a 24x7 basis while sources were deployed. Intensive analysis of the available interrogation reports of different gangsters was carried out to understand the spread of the alliance,' said Dhaliwal.

The SC was not just arresting gang members, he was also trying to get to the root of the problem. He discovered how the gangs worked and described it as a 'hub-and-spoke' model. He said that all the hubs were settled offshore and they were the links between gang members in India. Local members had minimal communication and spoke through superiors placed abroad, making their detection a herculean task. Intensive analytics found multiple foreign-based communication and coordination hubs in the UK, Canada, USA, Thailand, Malaysia, Armenia, Pakistan and other countries. Their local bases were concentrated in Bengaluru, Nasik, Zirakpur, Faridabad, Baddi, Delhi NCR and Dehradun.

While Moosewala was killed by local criminals, the plan to kill him was hatched at a much larger level.

Dressed in a langot, Lawrence Bishnoi sat on the floor facing a table and chair. He looked prepared to be interrogated for a serious crime. Dhaliwal was unfazed. The SC had questioned Lawrence earlier too. Dhaliwal, along with the Investigating Officer (IO), took a seat, not losing eye contact.

The IO glanced hard at the gangster and asked him to be ready for the harsh interrogation. Dhaliwal said, 'So, let's talk. We all know you guys did it, but why?'

Lawrence paused for a moment before he answered. 'Sir, have you heard his songs? Listen to them carefully and you will find out why.

'Vicky was my elder brother,' Lawrence said in a sharp whisper. 'He supported me and was my mentor. And they killed him.'

There was a glint of emotion in the hardened criminal's eyes. Lawrence now sat with his arms around his raised knees.

'He sang a eulogy for our rival, Bambiha. And the song's intro said it was not just a song but a slap on someone's face. We have responded to that slap. We had to safeguard our respect, our honour,' Lawrence said.

Later that night, Dhaliwal could not go to bed without listening to Moosewala's songs. He heard them all one by one, making notes, replaying bits to listen to certain portions again and again. He realised that a lot of what Moosewala had experienced was forever enshrined in his songs. To understand Moosewala and his point of view, it was important to understand his music.

By the time Dhaliwal finished, it was well past dawn. He had spent the night with Moosewala's music and it had given him some ideas as to why he had been killed. His teams had been working too, and had sent him lists of suspects. It was time to go after them.

NINE

THE INVESTIGATION

A blitzkrieg.

That was what the police investigation into Moosewala's killing had to be. Tracking killers on the run is always a dynamic situation, a race against time and all odds. In this case, the victim had been a high-profile singer and budding politician. So, the stakes were even higher. Public interest in the case was growing and the police knew that if they didn't get some answers soon, it would cast doubt on their ability to control crime. They worked furiously to solve the case and nab the fugitives. It wasn't easy given that the gang network was so widespread and underground.

Two separate state police teams were on the trail of the accused. On one side were the Punjab Police, led by DGP Gaurav Yadav, on the other were Special Commissioner H.G.S. Dhaliwal and the Delhi Police.

Both the police teams wanted to be the first to catch Moosewala's assailants. It was not just about grabbing headlines by solving a high-profile case. It was also about redeeming their reputation after their failure to prevent Moosewala's killing.

Less than 24 hours after the shoot-out, the Delhi Police picked up Rohit Moi, a sharpshooter and the defacto head of the Jitendra Gogi gang, on production remand from Tihar Jail. The cops believed he could have some information.

On the afternoon of 31 May, the Delhi Police got hold of Lawrence Bishnoi. The Punjab Police, too, had been planning to do the same, but the authorities in Delhi acted faster in getting him out of Tihar Jail on special remand.

Bishnoi would later move the Delhi High Court to seek protection against any decision to send him on remand to the Punjab Police. Why was he wary of the Punjab Police? In his statement to the court, Bishnoi pleaded that he not be handed over to the Punjab Police as he feared for his life.[1] There were several cases against him, and Bishnoi was afraid that authorities in Punjab might arrange an accident for him.

However, the authorities in Punjab weren't sitting idle as the police in Delhi interrogated Bishnoi. The Bolero that was used by the shooters had been found abandoned near the village of Khyala, close to the Punjab-Haryana border. On searching the vehicle, they found a fuel slip from a petrol pump in Fatehabad, Haryana. The slip was dated 25 May. A team from the Punjab Police rushed to the petrol pump and found CCTV footage of two of the shooters. The shooters had emerged from the Bolero to monitor the fuel metre while the attendant refuelled the car. In a bid to avoid being cheated by the staff, they ended up revealing their identities to the CCTV camera at the petrol pump. The two men were identified as Priyavrat Fauji and Kashish.

Later, ADGP Promod Ban claimed in interviews to media outlets that while they had identified the shooters from the CCTV footage, they had initially kept the information secret. 'We did not make it public as that would have cautioned the shooters and others,' he said.

The race between the two states and their police teams to be the first to solve the crime continued. The Delhi Police did not share information on the progress of the case, but the media kept reporting on it, attributing all information to reliable sources.

Though the shooters had taken care to diverge in their escape routes, the Delhi Police was able to establish a trail of their movements. Teams were dispatched towards Uttar Pradesh and Nepal, Madhya Pradesh and Pune. And yet another team went towards Gujarat, especially the Kutch region. Which trail would turn out to be the accurate one? It was an edge-of-the-seat thriller. On the seat sat Dhaliwal, keeping a close watch and following every lead, monitoring everything on his various devices, coordinating and guiding the teams on the ground while keeping his superiors informed.

Meanwhile, the Punjab Police was also under tremendous pressure. Firstly, it was widely known that the police had been aware of the threat Moosewala had been facing and yet, despite warnings, such a crime had taken place under their very noses. Secondly, since Moosewala had recently contested the elections (and lost), and the newly-formed AAP government had pruned his security, the killing was acquiring the proportions of a major political controversy. Thirdly, the government and the police feared an uprising of the masses. The crowd of mourners reaching Moosewala's house was growing every day.

If the Delhi and Punjab jurisdictions had worked together, perhaps the case would have been solved sooner; instead, the two teams concealed information from each other. The case was on every national media channel and both teams wanted to best the other. But who would finally win? Who would reach the shooters first?

<hr>

At its core, a crime scene can be viewed as a disassembled jigsaw puzzle. It takes a knowing hand to place the pieces together. Criminals may think they are brilliant, but mistakes happen during moments of inattention, and every criminal leaves behind some clues that are perceptible to the discerning eye.

For good investigators, every move of the criminals on the crime spot, every shoeprint, fingerprint even a strand of hair can be a clue. Then there are the bullets fired, the guns used, the mode of fire, the style of killing, the blood splatter, the route of escape, eyewitness accounts, blood samples—each of these can be a goldmine of information. It is little wonder then that cops survey the crime spot like ants swarming over food, looking at the minutest of details, examining every aspect of the area. In the Moosewala murder case, the very first clues and the most vital lead were the abandoned vehicles of the shooters—the Corolla and the Bolero. Who knew what secrets these cars contained?

⸺⸙⸺

A half-hour after Moosewala was shot at, AIG Chauhan of the Punjab Police was on his way to Mansa from Mohali. As his Innova sped along on its three-hour-long journey, Chauhan's mind raced with possibilities. Was Moosewala the victim of a gang war, as Goldy Brar had claimed in his post? Or was Brar's video a ploy to mislead the police? Was it a political murder? After Moosewala had lost the Assembly elections, which he had contested from Mansa just a few months ago, he had released a song titled *Scapegoat* cribbing about the betrayal of the Mansa voters. Moosewala's mother was the sarpanch of his village. Sarpanches often get involved in village disputes. Could that have something to do with his murder? Was it a case of personal enmity?

Or were terrorists involved? His song *295* had angered many, including religious leaders. The lyrics of the song openly challenged those who saw themselves as the sole custodians of the Sikh Panth. Moosewala sang: *Tu jhukeya zaroor ... thodda taan ni.*

> You may be down, but you have not submitted
> You still wear a turban,
> and have not shorn your hair
> I ask these self-styled dons of religion
> Is the Panth only theirs?

The song, which openly questions authority, became an instant hit with the youth, especially in Punjab and Kashmir. It struck a chord with those who were unhappy with the people in charge and became an anthem of sorts for disgruntled youth.

The song was named after Section 295 of the Indian Penal Code (IPC) which deals with offences related to hurting the religious sentiments. Moosewala had been at the receiving end of Section 295 when he was booked twice—on 1 February 2020 in Mansa, and then on 19 July 2020 in Mohali—for hurting the sentiments of the Sikhs though his song *Jatti Jeone Morh Vargi.*[2]

In the song, Moosewala invoked two historical characters—Jeona Morh, a dacoit in nineteenth-century Punjab, and Mai Bhago, who is hailed as a female warrior saint. Jeona Morh remains a popular character in Punjabi folk songs. A Robin Hood-like figure, he looted from the rich to feed the poor, and tales of his courage and generosity are familiar in Punjab.

Mai Bhago is revered as one of the great martyrs by the Sikhs. A feisty woman from Jhabal, Tarn Taran, the warrior played a key role in the historic battles fought by the Sikhs, led by Guru Gobind Singh, against the Mughals. In one such battle in the Malwa region of Punjab, forty soldiers deserted the Guru. Mai Bhago taunted these soldiers and motivated them to return to the Guru's side. According to the legend, a 10,000-strong Mughal army at Khidrana ki Dhab attacked the Sikhs led by Guru Gobind Singh. The forty soldiers led by Mai Bhago took on the army and chased them away. The soldiers achieved martyrdom and were hailed as the forty muktas. The place became famous as Muktsar Sahib.

In *Jatti Jeone Morh Vargi*, Moosewala sang about a strong female protagonist who never submits to anyone, quite like the gun of Jeona Morh. Popular Punjabi actress Sonam Bajwa acted in the video, which depicted her boldly taking on men and rescuing women from their clutches. In one of the verses, Moosewala likened her to Mai Bhago, rapping about how she had inherited the warrior-saint's nature. This did not go down well with some people. Two FIRs were filed against the singer for comparing a regular woman to Mai Bhago, a turbaned Amritdhari Sikh.

Though he apologised, Moosewala had his revenge by criticising the self-styled experts on religion and media in *295*. The song also took on his critics who flooded his social media channels with abusive comments. In it

Moosewala sang: *Oh gandiyan siyasatan … aisi date milugi*

> Expel dirty politics from your heart
> Leave someone fit to go to the Guru's house
> Otherwise, no child will have long hair
> Soon such a date will arrive

***

'Find everything you can about this Corolla,' Chauhan said in his messages to the field units. 'The registration number may be fake but we can still find something. Look at past cases involving gangsters where cars have been used. Talk to your informers, question gangsters in jails, ask residents of the village of Moosa if they had seen this kind of car earlier. Talk to your informers in the adjoining villages. Goddam it, ask everyone in Mansa, Bathinda, Barnala, the entire state, the entire country. Move heaven or hell. Just find something about this car,' Chauhan thundered at his team.

After Goldy Brar's interview with journalist Ritesh Lakhi—where he claimed responsibility for the killing of Moosewala—went live on the internet, cops in the state began working furiously. They had dug out dossiers on all the members of the Lawrence Bishnoi gang. Their supporters, underground workers and logistical aides were all on the police radar. People's phones were being tapped. Photos of suspects were shared on police WhatsApp groups and private communication channels of the departments. 'Look out for these people and get any information on them,' were the orders.

Finally, after all this frenetic activity, there was a glimmer of hope for the Punjab Police. One of the teams reported that an informer had seen gangster Manpreet Manna of Talwandi driving a Corolla some time ago. But Manna was in Faridkot jail. He had been in jail for about a year as an undertrial for the murder of a gangster named Kulbir Naruana. At the AGTF's behest, police of various districts initiated the paperwork necessary to bring him in for questioning from Faridkot. They also uncovered the fact that Manna was close to another gangster, Saraj Mintu, who had been shifted to Bathinda jail twenty days ago. 'They were close friends,' a jail official told the investigating AGTF. 'We had to put them in separate jails.' A production warrant was prepared for Saraj Mintu as well.

Mintu was a close aide of Jaggu Bhagwanpuria. The links were slowly forming—Bhagwanpuria and Lawrence were both in Tihar Jail, booked under MCOCA.

Chauhan and DSP Bikramjit Brar put all their energy into finding out more about Manpreet Manna, alias Manna Talwandi. He had been known to use the Corolla while on the run. An informer also tipped the police off that Manna was a relative of Bhau, who had been seen driving a Corolla as well. They were able to affirm that Manna Talwandi was the owner of a white Corolla. The clues were finally coming together.

Talwandi and Bhau, as well as Moosewala's shooters, seemed to be using the same Corolla.

When Bhau's phone was put on tracker, he popped up around Dehradun, some 300 km away from the area of the murder. 'Is this a deliberate attempt to be seen far away from the crime scene?' wondered Chauhan. 'It could be. It is a common modus operandi of such gangsters,' nodded Brar. A unit of the Bathinda AGTF rushed to Dehradun where Manna was caught the following day with the help of the Special Task Force (STF) of the Uttarakhand Police. Manna seemed surprised by his arrest. He had been roaming around in a white Scorpio with four friends. All of them were brought to Mansa immediately for questioning.

The fog engulfing Moosewala's murder had begun to clear. Bhau was a close aide of Manna. He was out on bail in a kidnapping and attempt to murder case. When pressurised by the police, he revealed that Manna Talwandi had got two Corollas delivered by Saraj Mintu. One of these had been given to Bhau to hand over to two persons at the Kotkapura Green Dhaba bypass, some 80 km northwest of Sidhu Moosewala's village.

The two persons who had received the car were Jagroop Singh Roopa and Mannu Kusa.

The Punjab Police noted their names carefully.

———

Dhaliwal's study table did not have even an inch of space. Every piece of paper, photograph, dossier and crime scene map associated with the Moosewala killing case was on it. There were carefully marked routes to Moosewala's house as well as routes away from the crime scene. Two of his teams were examining potential entry and exit routes. A separate team was looking at the CCTV footage. Yet another was trying to gather human intelligence associated with possible hideouts on the way used by the suspects. The police may be increasingly using technology to catch criminals but nothing beats the time-tested cultivation of informers. A Station House Officer (SHO) of any police station keeps such networks active and well-oiled. Such informers may be found among the criminal gangs too.

An interesting facet of the Indian police is how they can go into overdrive when necessary. They may fail to prevent a major crime from happening, but there is actually very little that they don't know. They have an extensive network of informers that they can tap into for information. In this case too, the Delhi Police activated informers within jails. News of almost all misdeeds, especially high-profile ones, circulate quickly in criminal circuits. As the Delhi Police reached out to rival gangs, they were able to make a significant breakthrough. Along with tracking phone and internet usage, TD analysis and intel from rival gangs, they were able to develop a visual profile of eight suspects in the case by 6 June. The images of these suspects were immediately splashed across the media. *The Hindustan Times* published photos and details of the men. Jagroop Roopa and Mannu Kusa featured in the poster, as did Priyavrat Fauji.

The fourth suspect was Harkamla Ranu of Bathinda's Parasaram Colony. Ranu was wanted in eleven criminal cases and had escaped police custody once already. The fifth suspect was Manjeet Bholu. Fauji's close associate, he belonged to the Kala Jathedia and Raju Basudi gang. He had also worked for Lawrence Bishnoi. Saurav Mahakal and Santosh Jadhav were the sixth and seventh suspects, both considered excellent marksmen. The eighth was Subash Banuda of Sikkar, Rajasthan. He was from the notorious Anandpal gang, active in the desert state of Rajasthan and part of the Lawrence Bishnoi syndicate.

Later investigations would reveal that only three of the eight suspects had been involved in the murder—Fauji, Mannu and Roopa. The involvement of the other five could not be established.

'We couldn't visit the crime spot or examine the body and bullets. We had to undertake this challenging detection with many handicaps due to our distance from the scene of crime as we wanted to ensure that our efforts were complementary to the investigating agency and that none of our actions in any way interfered with the work of the local police,' said H.G.S. Dhaliwal. 'We analysed the videos of the crime scene posted on social media. Based on the technical probe, the biggest break came when our teams shortlisted eight suspects. Of them, three proved correct and led to the cracking of the case.'[3]

On 6 June, the Punjab Police clinched a critical arrest. The CCTV footage from the front wall of Moosewala's house had shown several fans taking photos or selfies with the star as his Thar glided out slowly through the gates. One person was seen walking ahead of the Thar while taking pictures. That man was Sandeep, aka Kekda. He had been on a video call with Goldy Brar, providing him with real-time information about Moosewala's movements.

His photos were circulated, and inquiries were made of informers and villagers. One of the informers reported that he had seen Kekda many times in the last four days preceding Moosewala's murder. A witness, Sukhpal Singh Nambardar, mentioned in the police charge-sheet that he had seen Kekda in the house of one Jarnail Singh of the village of Moosa. Police soon learnt that Kekda was the son of Jarnail Singh's sister-in-law and he lived in the village of Kalanwali in Sirsa, Haryana.

The police raided his house and other possible hideouts in Bathinda and surrounding areas but Kekda eluded them. Meanwhile, an informer reported spotting him near the Guru Kashi University on the Bathinda-Dabwali road. Finally, the authorities had him in their grip.

The police were getting closer to solving the case. Kekda's arrest peeled away another layer behind which the killers hid. He cracked under police pressure and admitted that he, along with Baldev Nikku, another drug addict, had done a reconnaissance of Moosewala's house and his movements and sent information to Goldy Brar. Police recovered a sim card and an internet dongle from him. The clothes he had been seen wearing in the

CCTV recording were also found. In addition, his phone number and the call data records showed his location at the Moosewala feed tower, leaving no doubts as to his involvement.

Kekda remembered walking in front of Moosewala's car. 'It was not a car but a coffin on the road, I realised later,' he said during the interrogation. 'I didn't know they would kill him. I thought they would warn him or injure him or at most, break his bones, but to kill him in that way ... I didn't know ... I needed money for drugs. And big brothers [gangsters] protected me earlier in jail. But I only agreed to help as I needed money for drugs. I just wanted my dose ...' he told the AGTF officials.

⸻

Eventually, authorities in Punjab nabbed at least thirty-five criminals involved directly with the conspiracy to kill the singer. Additionally, around twenty-five others, it seemed, had been indirect participants related to other crimes.

Cops too were bewildered that sixty men, four of them in foreign countries, had come together to kill one man—Sidhu Moosewala.[4]

TEN

CATCHING THE SHOOTERS

With a solid list of suspects and leads in hand, it was time for the police to act. The syndicate was strong, the hideouts were many. The police now had to look for that one loose thread that could unravel the entire plot. Most gangsters are addicted to the same vices—alcohol, drugs and debauchery. Perhaps realising that such vices could become the weak point that could compromise their position, Lawrence Bishnoi and his gang members were known to keep away from drugs and women.

But the shooters involved in the case did not have such compunctions. All of them indulged in drugs and alcohol, and at least two of the six—Deepak Mundi and Ankit—were heavily dependent on them.

In Roopa and Mannu Kusa's case, it was 'chitta' that they could not do without. Named for its colour, chitta is a white powder drug that had become the new craze amongst the youth of Punjab. Derived from opium and laced with many chemicals, it is a cheaper alternative to heroin. The proliferation of this drug and its impact were depicted in the popular Hindi film *Udta Punjab*, featuring Shahid Kapoor and Alia Bhatt, which even had a song called *Chitta Ve*.

The chitta did Roopa and Mannu in.[1] They could not stay away from Punjab for too long as they were both dependent on the drug and needed to procure it regularly from their local sources. But before that, it was the de facto head of the shooters, Priyavrat Fauji, who got caught. Fauji's weakness for the pleasures of the flesh proved to be his undoing. He liked living on the edge; plotting a murder excited him and killing someone gave him an unmatched high. That was his primary drug. And then there were the women: he could never be satisfied with one. He always wanted more.

According to police officials, in the months prior to Moosewala's killing, Fauji had had four girlfriends. He had been unable to meet with them while he was busy preparing for the task he had been assigned. He could not meet them for a week after the murder either. It had been a while since he communicated with them and Fauji was getting restless.

Dhaliwal knew Fauji's primal instincts would soon get the better of him. Teams from the SC were already tracking the phones of the women connected to Fauji. Cops had obtained these numbers from human intelligence and the call data record of Fauji's phone identified from the tower dump.

By tracking the phones, the Special Police discovered Fauji talking to multiple women. Somehow, the fourth girlfriend, who had always suspected Fauji of being a philanderer, also found out about his womanising ways. 'Women just get to know,' quipped a police official with a grin and shrug while talking about the incident. The infuriated woman, whose identity the police has kept a secret, as they have the identities of Fauji's other girlfriends, contacted the SC with information on his whereabouts.[2]

By the time Fauji realised that his location had been compromised, it was too late. Police caught him and Kashish, alias Kuldeep, another shooter from Gujarat's Kutch district. They had been on the run together.

With the head of the Bolero module under arrest, it became easier to trace the others. Soon, Ankit was also caught. Fauji and Kashish's interrogation led the police to more hideouts and accomplices. The cops raided several places and tracked the people suspected of helping the gangsters. Their efforts soon bore fruit; they learnt that Ankit Sersa had contacted some 'friends' in New Delhi and was planning to hide in the NCR. He had been confident that he could hide in plain sight, but was arrested in North Delhi on 4 July, little more than a month after Moosewala's murder.

However, Roopa, Mannu and Deepak Mundi had disappeared. 'There were no traces anywhere. There was no electronic trail. They were out there among 130 crore Indians,' said one official, exasperated by the search.

Where were they? This was the question on everyone's lips.

ELEVEN

THE ENCOUNTER OF BONNIE AND CLYDE

20 JULY 2022

'It is Bonnie and Clyde. Confirmed. Move in,' DSP Bikramjit Singh Brar of the AGTF, Punjab, spoke into his walkie-talkie, delivering instructions to the Special Operations Group (SOG). The SOG had been formed in 2018, along the lines of the Israeli Commandoes. The impetus for it had been the two terror attacks in Punjab in 2016—one on a police station and another on an Air Force base. The SOG received specialised training from officers who had been trained by the Israeli army and police. In keeping with the style of the Israeli force, the SOGs are taught to strike at impossible targets with zero impact on themselves and civilians.[1]

The SOG commander waved at a group of four men to close in on a kothi that was situated amidst paddy fields on the outskirts of Bhakna Kalan, a village in the Tarn Taran district of Punjab, just 12 km short of the international border with Pakistan.

The city of Tarn Taran Sahib had been founded by the fifth Sikh Guru, Guru Arjan Devji, in the late sixteenth century. In a literal sense, Tarn Taran refers to a boat used to cross the ocean. However, the more spiritual interpretation of the name is that it is the boat used for crossing the ocean of existence. But for many criminal gangs and Sikh terrorist groups connected with Pakistan's Inter-Services Intelligence (ISI), Tarn Taran is a path to cross over from India to the neighbouring country. The barbed wire that runs throughout the 552 km across the international border with Pakistan acts as a barrier but is not always successful in preventing the smuggling and illegal crossing of people to and from the country. Despite the high security, there are numerous cases of people digging tunnels to either smuggle contraband items or slip past the Border Security Force.

⸺

DSP Brar, along with two police guards, moved towards the entrance of the kothi, while the SOG men crawled through the paddy fields towards the back of the house. Fifty-two days had passed since the killing of Sidhu Moosewala but the media was still tracking the story closely. Reports were constantly updating viewers about any progress in the case. Of the six shooters involved, the SC of the Delhi Police had arrested three—Fauji, Ankit and Keshav. The AGTF had not made any major breakthrough so far, arresting only the minor players, like the man who had provided the vehicles for the murder. They knew they had to show some results soon. Top officials of the AGTF, including its chief, Promod Ban, AIG Gurmeet Singh Chauhan and DSP Bikramjit Singh Brar were personally monitoring all the human and technical intelligence. It was only on 10 July that they finally got reliable information about the movements of the suspects at Bhakna Kalan.

Bonnie and Clyde—the names of an infamous American criminal couple—were the code names of Roopa and Mannu Kusa, who had managed to evade the police so far. Roopa and Mannu were not a couple, but according to DSP Brar, the way they had just disappeared from the scene had made the police choose these code names for them.

The two were a part of the Corolla module of shooters. Barely an hour after shooting at Moosewala's car, Roopa and Mannu Kusa fled in a stolen Alto. They then headed towards Barnala, northwest of the crime spot. They knew that police would soon be alerted to what had happened and raise the security levels, so they took the village link roads to avoid the police nakabandis. By 9 p.m., they had travelled about 80 km to reach the town of Raikot. All this while, they had remained in touch with Goldy Brar through the Signal app, using an international sim card and an internet dongle. Mannu's aunt lived in Raikot and the two men rested for the night at her house.

The next day, they abandoned the Alto near Makhu. In a different car now, they first reached Moga but then, on receiving some instructions from Goldy Brar, turned back and went towards Harike Barrage where the Sutlej River swells in size after a confluence with the Beas River some 10 km upstream. This is where several barrages stop the further flow of water into Pakistan, forming the largest manmade wetland in northern India, the Harike Wetland, with the Harike Lake in the deeper part of it. Under the Indus Water Treaty with Pakistan, India has rights over Sutlej, Beas and half of the waters of the Ravi River, while Pakistan gets its share from the other half of Ravi, along with Chenab and Jhelum.

The wetland is called a 'mand', the Punjabi term for marshy land. There are some islands here and small peninsulas as well, making it a perfect hiding place for fugitives. Roopa had chosen a slightly isolated island to be their next hideout. The two reached via boat and found a hut to stay in. They had been on the island for almost two weeks before Roopa's stash of drugs ran out.

'It was the need for drugs that did them in,' said DSP Brar. 'When the uncontrollable craving for drugs is triggered, it is like some tentacles have grown in your intestines and are squeezing them. You have to feed drugs to this demon. Your brain doesn't function. It only keeps thumping on repeat—drugs, drugs, drugs. You sweat and your limbs are twisted. Roopa had to move out.'

Mannu Kusa was also addicted to intoxicants but more to capsules and pills. He could still manage, but Roopa was desperate for chitta. He had his sources, and he often went out to score drugs, bringing stuff back for himself and for Mannu.

'We had been hunting for them but could not find their tracks anywhere. Then we recalled Roopa's addiction to drugs. We activated our informants in that trade. Soon information started trickling in,' said DSP Brar. 'We found that a duo with similarities to Roopa and Mannu had been spotted in Jandiala. CCTV footage from a shop in Moga district showed the two suspects riding a bike on 10 July. They were moving towards Tarn Taran. The last information we received was from the village of Bhakna Kalan, 12 km from the international border. Were they planning to run to Pakistan?'

In the early hours of 20 July, Brar received information that the two men could be hiding in an isolated house outside the village of Bhakna Kalan. 'The local unit and the SOG men were called in,' said Brar.

And that was how the AGTF and the SOG found themselves in the paddy fields of Bhakna Kalan, surrounding the house where the two were hiding. DSP Brar spoke into a megaphone, asking Roopa and Mannu to surrender. In response, a barrage of bullets was fired from inside the kothi. That was it. The cops unleashed their bullets on the gangsters.

The exchange of fire between the police and the two shooters went on for almost two hours. Roopa and Mannu climbed up on the roof of the house, with Roopa perched on a beam, firing with his AK-47 at any movement in the fields. A stray bullet hit a media person from a TV channel.[2]

The SOG acted fearlessly. Nearly twenty men inched closer to the building despite facing incessant fire from the two shooters, who were clearly not ready to give up. Soon four hours had elapsed. Tired of the lengthy encounter, Brar ordered snipers to target Mannu, who was on the roof. He then directed another group of the SOG sharpshooters to break down the wall that covered the stairs where Roopa was firing from. The SOG fired continuously at the wall that shielded the gangster, rupturing it and finally hitting Roopa. Shortly afterwards, a sniper hit Mannu. After a long and heavy exchange of fire which had injured three policemen along with a mediaperson, Roopa and Mannu Kusa—Moosewala's murderers and dreaded members of the Bhagwanpuria gang—were finally dead.

The picture of Roopa's body, collapsed on the beam above the stairs with his gun next to him, went viral. Police officials recovered two mobile phones from the bodies. The phone forensics team were able to trace the duo's movements prior to this day. Priyavrat Fauji and the others arrested had already revealed that their plan had been to run away from Punjab, hide in Gujarat for some time and then find a way to reach Nepal. But Roopa had believed his hideouts in Punjab would keep him safe for some time. After that, he had planned to cross the international border into Pakistan where gangster-turned-terrorist Rinda could help him. Now, however, Roopa lay dead, mourned by no one.

Roopa had been disowned by his family when he had chosen the criminal way of life. His parents remained publicly stoic, expressing no sympathy for their dead son. His mother, Palwinder Kaur, blamed the government for the increased drug abuse and unemployment in the state that led many young people to choose a life of crime.

Mannu still had people to mourn him after his death. Residents of the village of Kusa, where he had lived with his family, remembered the 'soft-hearted' village carpenter who had always spoken kindly to everyone. That had been before circumstances changed him forever.[3]

THE MOTHER

'He may be Sidhu Moosewala to the world, but to me, he will always be Gaggu. That's what I called him when I held him for the first time,' said Charan Kaur. 'His voice sounded so sweet. Of course, a child's voice always sounds sweet to its mother but everyone who heard him speaking and singing compared him to the forgotten melons which once grew in abundance in Moosa. They told me his name and fame would spread far and wide like the sarda's fragrance.'

There had been a time when villagers from Moosa grew sarda in abundance. These were quite popular and much in demand not just locally but also in places as far away as Delhi and Mumbai.

'Melons were to Moosa what oranges are to Nagpur. The fruit was known by various names. Sarda, sharda, kachhre and the local popular name, chibbadd. The city-dwellers call it kharbuja or melon,' said Dr Sukhpal Singh, a leading agro-economist of Panjab Agricultural University (PAU), Ludhiana.

Joginder Singh Mann, a journalist with the *Punjabi Tribune*, who covered the Mansa district for the paper, recalled how, as a child, he would feast on the melons and see traders from 'big cities' coming to the village for an advance deal. 'In Mumbai and Gujarat, the sarda from Moosa was always in high demand,' he says.

Perhaps some of the sweetness of the sarda of Moosa seeped into the voice of Charan Kaur's young son. But the nature of the land was changing. The once abundantly grown fruit became increasingly scarce in the region, before disappearing altogether. Moosewala too was no longer just the boy with a sweet voice. As his fame grew, his lyrics changed into brazen boasts about himself and his caste—the Jats. He often threatened his enemies in his songs and made bold statements against the lack of tolerance of religious leaders. Perhaps it was the rebelliousness of youth, but Moosewala started to use his voice to talk about societal, cultural or religious norms that he found oppressive.

His music became his cry for freedom.

Charan had always been a big influence on the singer. Moosewala had fond childhood memories of listening to his mother sing the Gurbani while oiling and combing his hair.

In an interview with Punjabi actress and TV host Sonam Bajwa, Moosewala said, 'Even now, my mother combs my hair before a big show. It is a bond every mother and son have, or should have.'[1] On 14 May, Moosewala paid tribute to his mother on her birthday by releasing the song *Dear Mama*—his love and adulation are evident in each word of the song. The song revealed a tender side to the man whose entire public persona was otherwise one of unfettered machismo. In the song, Moosewala raps about how his temper is hot and can blaze like the sun, but at other times, he is calm and serene like the dawn. And when he is like that, he is just like his mother. He also reflects that he is, at times, angry at the world like his father, but then the calmer and more compassionate side of him prevails. He sings: *Kade suraj wangu ... tere warga aa.*

> Sometimes I burn like the sun
> At other times I am at peace
> Like the dawn
> Mother, I always feel
> I am just like you
>
> Sometimes like my father
> I feel angry at the world
> But then, every time, like you
> I, too, feel pity for the world
>
> Some say my face is like this
> Some say my face is like that
> But my face is just like yours

Mother, I always feel
I am just like you

Two days after Sidhu Moosewala's funeral, Charan held her son's ashes in an urn. The grief-stricken mother could be heard repeating to herself, 'You've reduced my strapping son to ashes in this pot. You think you will get peaceful sleep?'

Later, Charan appeared in different videos at the memorial constructed at the site where the singer's last rites had been held. 'My son was an engineer. He could have settled anywhere he wanted, even before he earned fame as a singer. He rejected a Permanent Residency in Canada to settle in the village as he respected his roots. He loved his parents and loved mother earth. Someday, he will return again ...'[2]

THIRTEEN

THE MAN AND THE SINGER

Sidhu Moosewala, as the world knew him, was very different from Shubhdeep, that only close friends and family knew. According to the singer Amrit Mann, who often co-wrote songs with him, and his financial manager Bunty Bains, so different were the two personas that it was like knowing two different people. Mann and Bains worked closely with Moosewala and gradually got to know the singer better than most others in the industry.

'We all have different public and private lives, but for Sidhu, the two personalities were like the opposing poles of our planet. What one saw in front of the camera was the singer; the real man only emerged in private,' said Bains. 'Unlike his robust, macho, gun-wielding persona in his songs and videos, Sidhu was actually quite shy, and would rarely open up to people. Despite his big presence in the studio—physically and because of his stature in the industry—he spoke softly and sweetly, and hardly ever raised his voice. Mostly, he would talk with his head bent and eyes lowered, but then, mid-conversation, he would raise his head to make a point and at that moment, you could peek into his mind and soul.'

'I heard Moosewala's first song *G-Wagon* while waiting to board a flight at the New Delhi international airport. The song mesmerised me immediately ... Later, in Canada, I saw Moosewala and shook hands with him. I said, you sing and write *ghaint* (superb). You have a spark. Nurture and strengthen it,' Mann recalled. After a pause, his voice breaking, he added, 'Who knew that five years down the line, I would be trying to find him in this pot of ashes? And hugging his lifeless statue made of stone?'

For Moosewala, his close friends were his *jaan*, his heart and his life. Bains remembered how he had once been discussing the lyrics of a song with the rapper and suggested some improvements, to which Moosewala replied, 'Okay, *jaan*.' 'I noticed his innocence,' said Bains. Later, he called Bains to clarify that that was how he addressed his close friends. 'We had just begun working together ... The way of address became popular among the music fraternity and we sometimes addressed each other as "*jaan*". The word strengthened our bond.'

Sidhu was also affectionately called Giani by some. 'Giani' is what a learned turbaned Sikh is addressed as.

Ironically, that was the name the killers used for Sidhu in their coded conversation.

As a child, Shubhdeep was known to have a sweet voice, but he only sang his first song in public when he was about eleven. It was a religious song that he sang at a school function. After that, he sang many times off and on.

His cousin, Arshdeep Singh, who works as a physical education teacher in a government school in Ahmedgarh, remembers their shared childhood days fondly. 'Shubhdeep, my younger brother and I used to study in Sarvhitkari Vidya Mandir, Mansa. I was a year senior to them,' he said. Arshdeep recalled that Moosewala would ride 11 km to school and back on his bicycle every day. 'A school van used to go to the village to pick and drop off students, but Shubhdeep's father didn't have money to pay for the service. Hence, Shubhdeep pedalled to the school and back in all sorts of weather. And he never forgot his humble beginnings. That is why he wanted a senior school, a hospital and a stadium in the village,' he said.

Shubhdeep was part of the school bhangra team and captain of the kabaddi team. Arshdeep's brother, Sukhmandeep Singh, was a member of the kabbadi team too. The cousins were very close. 'My brother settled in Calgary, Canada. When I got married mid-May, Shubhdeep and my brother danced together. We all had dinner together on the night of 25 May, four days before the murder. The next day, my brother flew to Canada and Shubhdeep promised to see him soon as he had a show in Calgary in June. That day never came ... My brother passed into depression and locked himself in his room after he heard of Shubhdeep's death. He died nine days later of a heart attack,' said Arshdeep.

Shubhdeep was proud of his education. In media interviews, he would talk about being one of the few in his village who had an engineering degree.[1] 'I have seen my parents work hard for me. They were worried that, like many youths in the state, I may get involved with drugs or other illegal activities in some way, but I was committed to making a name. So, I tried engineering and got good marks and a seat at GNE Ludhiana [Guru Nanak Dev Engineering College], among the best colleges in the country. Engineering was to make a living, but music was the food for my soul. That is why I tried my hand at music again when I was in Ludhiana.'

Shubhdeep's passion for singing seems to have really developed when he was studying engineering. He started taking lessons from Harvinder Bittu, a music teacher who had a school near the industrial city of Ludhiana.

'Sidhu first came to me sometime in 2014. I think he was in the third year of his engineering course,' recalled Bittu. 'He was what we call in local parlance a *shreef jeha munda*, a shy, polite and well-mannered boy. He rarely talked, just a word or two here and there. Later, I would be surprised by the aggression in his songs and stage performances. That was someone else. The one who came to learn music was Shubhdeep Singh from a village in a backward region of Punjab. And it seemed he was not very confident in the urban competitive world. But people change, thinking changes and the company you keep also changes. The person I saw in those music videos was not Shubhdeep. He was Sidhu Moosewala.'

When he first met him, Bittu liked the youngster's voice but found him raw. 'He had an innocent freshness which teachers love, as they can shape the singer. Sidhu learnt vocal, harmonium and tumbi in school,' said Bittu. 'He was very keen and hardworking, but no one can make you a singer. No one can gift you a voice and control. He had something, but music comes to you on its own. You can't learn it in a laboratory. He wasn't promising at first, but then music found him. The real change came when he went to Canada. He was a different person, a star.'

Bittu recalls that Shubhdeep wrote his first song, *License*, while still in music school. 'He trained for almost a year. Once he became confident, he wanted to sing his own songs. We found a songwriter and had some sessions with him. However, the writer didn't deliver the songs despite assurances. That upset Sidhu and he announced that he would write his own songs.'

Arshdeep added, 'A songwriter promised Sidhu he would write, but he didn't. The man was not answering his phone calls. So, a day before the scheduled recording of the song, Sidhu went to the man's house in a village in Ludhiana though it was late in the evening and it was raining. When Sidhu reached his house, the writer sought money for the song. "I don't have any money to pay. I even rode my bike to your house on borrowed petrol," Sidhu told him. That was our Sidhu. He was not cowed down by things. Later, when he found his partners would not pay him equally, he started his own music label.'

Now that Shubhdeep had decided to write his own song, he needed a fitting subject. The conversation with his friends and his teacher led to the story of Shaheed Udham Singh of Sunam, a town not too far from Moosewala's home district of Mansa. Udham Singh had killed General Michael O'Dwyer, a former Lt. Governor of Punjab during British rule, on 13 March 1940, in London, to avenge the Jallianwala Bagh massacre that took place on 13 April 1919. Bittu recalled drawing Shubhdeep's attention to the fact that Udham Singh had waited for more than twenty years to finally get his revenge. Moosewala's eyes had lit up listening to the tale and he said, 'It is amazing that he kept the spirit of revenge alive for so long, but I wonder how he got a licence in England to carry that gun.' Bittu chuckled and said, 'Who needs a licence when you know your mission will end in certain death for you?'

Those words seem to have resonated with Shubhdeep and he wrote the song *License* which was released in June 2016. Punjabi singer Ninja sang it while Gold Boy composed the music. It was released by Speed Records. It said: *Jinhe chakna … licence nahiyo lainde.*

> The brave do not need a warrant
> To raid the enemy's house
> Or a licence to use weapons
> Their guts are enough

Through his first song, Shubhdeep was making a statement. According to Bittu, Moosewala wanted to proclaim his arrival on the scene through his lyrics. He wanted people to sit up and take notice. 'Sometimes, people from small cities and unknown villages overdo things just to convey that they are also there, that they also matter and they are something. I think Sidhu wanted to simply tell the world that he was someone too. That he and his family had laboured hard, which most families do in one way or the other. And that he had risen from humble origins,' Bittu said.

In his later songs too, Moosewala sang about historical characters, local Robin Hoods, gangsters, terrorists and militants. Bittu noticed his attraction towards rebels and heroes, both historical and from folklore. Some of those 'heroes' were considered exactly that by the state. Bittu said, 'With times, *kalakars* change. They play to the gallery. I felt Shubhdeep's lyrics came from deep within. He later learnt about the market, and I think that changed him, or maybe it was the different kind of company he began to keep. At the same time, you have to notice that many singers die in penury while saving Punjabi boli and idiom in their art, whether in songs or stories. Why should Moosewala have met the same fate?' It was true that people loved Moosewala's brand of Punjabiyat—the masculine bravado, the guns, the fast cars and the gumption to fearlessly take on one's enemies. It pushed Sidhu to play up that part of his personality.

Bittu feels it would have been better if Moosewala had kept his teachers and old friends close. 'I understand he was busy and had moved to different levels, but your first teachers and friends keep you grounded. Unlike professional friends, they tell you to your face if you are wrong.'

But it wasn't like Moosewala forgot his friends and music guru. 'Yes, he mentioned me in many interviews until 2018. Later, he got busy, and I think the media also wanted him to talk about controversies and music rather than his journey. I last saw him in person on my birthday in December 2016. After that, he went to Canada. I believe something drastic happened to his psyche and his persona in Canada. In Punjabi, we have a word called *"mandeer"*, which means a footloose group of youth who don't care much for the law. *Mandeer* in Punjab are like the "hoods" in Western countries. Moosewala had become a part of the *mandeer*. I heard some fight or dispute took place between him and his friends in Canada that made him come back,' Bittu said.

Moosewala's return from Canada to his small village was often discussed in media interviews. He and his parents spoke about his return to his roots. 'I did not accept the Permanent Residency of Canada. I wanted to do something for the village I was born in. I wanted to tell the world that if one is on the right path, one can live and grow in one's village. When I see the mad rush among the youth to migrate to Canada, the UK or other places, I want them to look at me and believe that anything is possible living in India, close to your parents, your responsibilities and your roots,' said Moosewala.[2]

There was another reason, though. Moosewala left Canada immediately after the Canadian police banned his shows following clashes.[3]

Raghuraj, a Chandigarh-based architect who designed and constructed Moosewala's haveli in the village of Moosa, remembers the singer's insistence on Punjabi architecture. 'He used to live with his parents in a two-room house. The approach road and the house started to feel cramped as his following grew. Then, he decided to construct a haveli on the outskirts of the village, but didn't want it to be modern.'

The architect recalled that Moosewala wanted tall walls with traditional Punjabi-cum-Rajasthani designs and elephant-sized doors in heavy teakwood gilded with brass. But the interior was designed like a simple Punjabi haveli. At the back were living rooms, with the drawing room and kitchen on either side facing a large courtyard. In the open verandah, Shubhdeep and his father would often lie on a cot, talking or relaxing. The singer had wanted to popularise Punjabi haveli architecture with its projections and *jharokhas*. 'I stand for bringing youth back to their villages, back to farming and back to being proud of the Punjabi language. Then how can I build a modern home?' he reasoned.

—◆—

Professor Khushdeep Singh, Shubhdeep's teacher in college, remembers him as one of the shyest students he had ever seen. 'It is common for students to approach teachers for relaxation in viva voce exams, but Shubhdeep never came to me for that. Of course, you can't say he was timid or underconfident, but he was humble and never indulged in any fight, argument or misbehaviour that was so common among college students.'

Jagroop Singh Jarkhar, a journalist with the newspaper *Ajit*, was present at one of the college annual functions and heard Moosewala sing. 'He sang a song of *Yamla Jatt*. He was okay. It was not that remarkable that students would ask him to sing more. But later, when we saw him in the music videos, he had become an established professional singer.'

Professor Singh had a son studying in the US who later introduced him to the new Moosewala. 'My son kept telling me there is a new Punjabi singer who the youngsters are especially mad about. And that he'd said in an interview he had studied at GNE college.'

Professor Singh said he was surprised when he saw Shubhdeep in the avatar of Sidhu Moosewala. 'The shy, humble guy was brandishing guns, challenging his adversaries, roaming the "hood". He was even indulging in verbal exchanges with his so-called enemies on social media and in interviews. He was not the Shubhdeep we knew. Canada had changed him. There was a new consciousness, it seemed,' he said.

Parminder Singh, a radio journalist and Punjabi talk show host, said in one of his programmes, that through his songs, Sidhu Moosewala discusses Sikh immigrants and their identity in Brampton. 'His song *B-Town* is a tribute to the place where Sikh migrants, many from humble backgrounds like his, made their mark. His songs about this identity resonated with the youth.'

Parminder also spoke about Moosewala's time in Canada. 'He began his career in Canada, was doing amazing … for folks who come to Canada, this was like, we've made it, and we're going to get settled here,' Parminder said, implying that Moosewala's songs became a symbol of grit and determination for the migrant Punjabis.

Eminent professor of political science and columnist Ronki Ram wrote in *Outlook* magazine, 'Asked why he kept his eyes downward while interacting with interviewers even though he thundered on the stage, his reply used to be: "Well, in my personal and social life, I am like that, whereas on stage, I need to play to the gallery professionally."It was for such rooted traits that Moosewala became a legend across caste, class, creed and regional boundaries.'[4]

Amrit Mann, who worked closely with Moosewala, said the efforts to understand the singer and his lyrics will continue. 'When we used to compose and sing, we wondered about the lyrics—but not too much. But now that he has left us as suddenly as he arrived on the music scene, you understand his songs or, at least, you get some hint of what he was singing about.'[5]

Death, it seems, was a constant motif in Moosewala's work and music.

'Look at the lyrics—*layi firda ... phere* (he is wedded to death)—in the song *Bambiha Bole*. When I saw his body with the bridal sehra around his head, I recalled that line. He had actually wedded death at a young age. Who was this man, I wonder,' Mann said.

'Who could have thought about the song *The Last Ride*? Who talks about coffins in their youth? I wonder in which zone of awareness he was when he wrote and sang those songs. I remember uncle and aunty [Sidhu's parents], especially his mother, objecting to the lyrics in vain,' Mann recalled.

Did he really know he would die young? 'I think he did,' Mann states. 'It was something coming from deep within. Perhaps some deeply evolved souls know their future. What was that power within him which got the song released days before he left us? There has to be some compelling energy within him or in this universe which drove him to talk about death. Many now say he knew about his end, that his life would be short. Yes, that is what the songs say. Yes, that is what has dawned upon us after his death.' Mann's voice trailed off and he stared into the distance. Moosewala had taken away all the answers with him.

FOURTEEN

MOOSEWALA'S LIFE AND LYRICS

To know Moosewala, one has to know his songs. The visceral lyrics are honest and hide nothing. Through them, the singer, shy as he was in real life, expressed himself. 'I write my songs based on my experiences. When I sing a song in a live programme like this, there is a reel playing in my mind about the time or the circumstances when I wrote those particular lines. Like, I just sang *Legend* and you think about something while hearing it but in my mind, the reel of the time when I wrote and composed it plays in the background,' said Sidhu Moosewala on 31 January 2020, while performing at the annual Basant Mela at Baoli Baba Bhandari ji in the Hoshiarpur district of Punjab.[1] Set in the foothills of the Dhauladhar range of the great Himalayas, it is one of the most notable traditional melas in Punjab.

The singer was in his element that evening. He sang from his core but more importantly, he spoke from his heart in between performing songs on public demand. He hinted at how his rivals tried to pin him down. 'But they were mistaken to think they had succeeded. Pygmies,' he said, scoffing at his rivals in the music industry.

While his songs remain open to interpretation, perhaps no one will ever be able to explain their true meaning. His words on the stage at the Basant Mela have been analysed, interpreted and re-interpreted several times after his death.

As lead organiser of the event, Parminder Bariana witnessed the live show. 'People, including me, screamed in appreciation and sang and laughed with him, thinking his monologues between the songs were part of the performance, but that was not the case. Only now, after his brutal killing, we realise what was possibly going on in his mind. The video of that song has been shared a number of times after his murder, with fans commenting that he hinted at people harassing him.'

The song during which he launched into a tirade on stage is called *Hathyar*. It was released in July 2019 under The Kidd music label and has over 50 million views to date. It was part of the album *Sikander 2*, released worldwide in August 2019. 'The game is not over yet. He is back to finish it,' appears in bold lettering on the screen at the beginning of the video, with his trademark

'*Aw dil da ni maara*, Sidhu Moosewala' (You may dislike him but Sidhu Moosewala is not a man with a bad heart) blaring in the background. In *Hathyar*, Moosewala sings: *Sadde kolo seham ... udaariyan laun lage.*

> People who were once scared to even look at us
> I hear have now started to challenge us,
> trying to grab our collar
> Seeing that the sky looks empty
> The flock of partridges are trying
> to fly high like eagles

Moosewala used words like '*titran*' (partridges) and snakes for his enemies and rivals in his songs. In Punjabi, '*titar*' is used to refer to a weak person who can be easily caught and eliminated. Moosewala's music and songs are rooted in the Punjabi way of life. He used his music to talk about the machoism of the Jats and their courage. Using rural imagery, he made fun of his rivals, comparing them to tempos. Large three-wheelers, called *maruta* in rural parlance, tempos are run on engines which are sometimes hand-started. So the driver keeps the engine running at chowks, lest the vehicle stops. Moosewala was implying that his rivals were running idle in one place, like the tempo, and not going anywhere.

A recurrent theme in his songs is that of a macho Jat, who is ruthless with his enemies, but is kind-hearted. Or a gangster, seemingly tough and unflinching in the face of danger, but principled enough to never harm the innocent and be gentle with children and women. The image of the central character is one of fearless bravado. In Moosewala's videos we see weapons being brandished freely, bloodshed, cars flying around and a master gangster with his entourage of bodyguards, who follow at a distance, scared to be too close to the boss.

Social commentator Ajay Pal Singh Brar, who participated in the year-long farmers' agitation, among other social movements, terms this bold expression of hypermasculinity typical of Punjabi youth. 'His songs on scaring our rivals hypes up our own masculinity. Moosewala kept himself high and so did his listener. This hypermasculinity is like a kick from Red Bull or cocaine. His lyrics give you a rush. For the youth of Punjab, who have been directionless since the days of terrorism, Moosewala's songs gave them the adrenaline rush they longed for. Can we blame them? As a society, we have failed to give our youth better goals. They need a higher purpose in life.'

Pune-based writer, speaker and entrepreneur Amit Bamzai wrote, 'I heard about Sidhu three years back when I was checking out a Marshall speaker in an electronics store. To say that I was hooked by the addictive bass and masculine language of his song "Old Skool" would be an understatement. The whole song is an unadulterated manifestation of aspirational Punjabi youth that is aware of its masculinity and doesn't shy away from flaunting either its "kaal Range Rover" or its double-barreled rifle or, as it is popularly known in Punjab, "dunali". As I played this song on a loop in my car while I drove every day to work, I feel no shame in admitting that it gave me the necessary gusto to handle the uncertainties of my entrepreneurial world.'[2]

The lyrics Bamzai mentions are: '*Ho mukeya ni ... kar gaur balliye.*'

> Listen, I am not finished
> Look at my status and reputation
> I walk with cops around me
> I am not made for some girl,
> I am made for guns.
> This Jatt has brought about a revolution.
> Pay attention.

Moosewala courted trouble more than once for his songs. In 2020, police lodged four different FIRs against him for glorifying weapons, promoting gun culture and violence and illegally firing an AK-47. The charges included performance of obscene acts and songs, disobedience to a (government) order and provocation to break the peace.[3]

'Yes, I talk about weapons for I believe keeping a gun is good if it is for your safety. But otherwise, it is not good. I am accused of promoting gun culture and violence. But don't they see films like *RRR* or Hollywood films which thrive on violence, gory murders and bloodshed? The Indian government doesn't book these filmmakers for inciting violence. Why only Moosewala?'⁴ the singer said in an interview a few weeks before his death.

'If you think keeping and brandishing guns is an act of violence, then why is there a provision for getting an arms licence? Stop issuing arms licences. Act against the censor board which cleared my songs and which clears other songs or films that show guns, gangsters and violence,' he argued.

Upset at the police cases and mounting criticism, Moosewala lamented that he was the most judged among his contemporaries. 'I don't understand this one-sided action. I don't talk about drugs or liquor which others do. Some first sing about drugs, then they participate in de-addiction drives to earn the government's favour. These people are hypocrites. I don't do that. I have not plucked my eyebrows like several nor shorn my hair and then claimed to be a champion of the religion like other Sikh singers. It is fair to believe that they think they can fail me by criticising me but they can only try. *Badnaam kar sakde ho nakaam nahi* (You can defame me but you cannot make me fail).'

Harjinder Thind, noted radio journalist in Canada, asked Moosewala in an interview: 'Your critics say your songs are making gangsters of the youth. That you always glorify weapons and keep a gun ...'

Moosewala defended himself. 'Is it the first time that a singer is talking about weapons and rivals? It is rooted in our culture. Punjab has been braving invaders since time immemorial. Punjabis were the wall each invader first confronted before marching to Delhi or mainland India. We were the defenders. We also fought against oppression if someone occupied our territory. These courageous tales are in our folklore, in our blood. But my critics don't appreciate that I have not glorified the use of drugs and liquor or showcased girls in provocative dresses.'[5]

On 24 May 2022, Akal Takht Jathedar Giani Harpreet Singh kicked up a controversy by asking all Sikhs to keep licenced weapons. While all political parties, barring the SAD, criticised the announcement, Sidhu Moosewala fully supported the Jathedar. 'It is the need of the hour. The Jathedar has asked for licenced weapons as Punjab is a border state and if some day we have to fight intruders, we should at least have the weapons to do so. And the Jathedar has asked us to take a licence for the weapons, which means he is abiding by the law of the land. What is the harm in it?'[6]

Incidentally, Punjab has the third-highest number of arms licences while Uttar Pradesh tops the list. According to statistics released by the home ministry, as on 31 December 2016, Uttar Pradesh had more than 12 lakh licences and Punjab had about 3.6 lakh. However, on the licence–people ratio, 0.63 per cent of the population in UP owned a licence compared to 1.3 per cent of Punjab.[7] In 2019, seeing the mad rush of applications for arms licences in Ferozepur, IAS officer Chander Gaind came up with a unique plan to benefit the environment. He made it mandatory for every licence holder to plant ten saplings and submit selfies with the plants as proof to be eligible for a licence.

Moosewala insisted a licenced weapon was not dangerous for the state. 'I don't understand why the Election Commission [of India] asks people to deposit all licenced weapons in a police station before elections. How many murders have taken place with such weapons? It is the illegally kept weapons which cause gory murders and law and order problems.' His statement in favour of arms licences invited more criticism.

Just four days later, six shooters gunned him down with sophisticated but illegal weapons.

One can see the singer's thought process evolve through the lyrics of his songs. Seen through the prism of his life in the village and the political situation in Punjab, his lyrics tell the tale of a young and reckless mind growing into a mature one, a mind concerned with social change.

Perhaps the greatest loss in all this is that Moosewala was killed just when he had begun to call for change. Analysing Sidhu's lyrics over his short career, one can see a shift away from the themes of Jat supremacy, hypermasculinity and gun culture that were an integral part of his earlier songs. Moving away from the popular tropes, he had started singing about Punjab's socio-political issues, such as political prisoners. 'The fruit of his music was about to ripen when it was plucked away,' said Sukhdarshan Natt, a senior leader of the Punjab

Kisan Union. 'We did not allow any singer or artist to make speeches from the stage of the agitation ... Like others, he composed songs on our plight. His was nearer to our hearts as he was a farmer's son and tilled his land himself. If you look at his songs *295* and *SYL*—the second released after his demise—you will notice that these songs were not about himself or his enemies, these were about enemies of the state, social issues and the sufferings of people.' His admiration for militant figure Jarnail Singh Bhindranwale was not hidden, but he had also been tagging the extremists as *dharm ke thekedars*, or self-proclaimed custodians of the faith. Moosewala vented his ire on the *dharm ke thekedars* in *295*.

Chamkaur Singh, Moosewala's paternal uncle, who has seen both good and bad times with the family, points out that Moosewala's music and lyrics were evolving. 'His early songs were all about the demands of the gallery as well as his own rant against his rivals and enemies. He used rural metaphors to silence his rivals, to make fun of them but he had progressed to churning out lyrics that spoke of bigger issues. He had started commenting on how a few people had become self-styled authorities on Sikhism or any religion, and how the state did not allow the airing of different views and instead suffocated opposing or critical voices.'

The singer was slowly coming into his own as a performer and cultural figure, writing not just popular hits but songs that spoke to the times. He may have been a shy person once, but he understood his audience well and was beginning to use his position to take to them ideas and issues that mattered to him. Like all great performers, he knew how to connect with his audience. Writer Ronki Ram observed, 'Another aspect of his being attached to the communitarian tradition of the culture at the grassroots was the way he used to address the audience during the concerts. He is known for greeting ladies and gentlemen as behnas and matas (sister and mothers) and bhravans and buzurgs (brothers and venerable elders), respectively. At times, he was heard requesting the huge gatherings at his akharas to take extra care when leaving the halls to reach home safely with special concern for the care of children. In one of his many earlier videos that turned viral after his ghastly murder, he can be seen consoling a weeping child who had been slapped by someone. He motivated him not only to laugh but also to recite a few lines of one of his many hits—*uchiyan ne gallan tere yaar diyan*.'[8]

At the Basant Mela in Hoshiarpur, Moosewala had captured the attention of the audience. He addressed them as brothers and sisters and mothers and elders, in his signature style. He even greeted a photojournalist, thanking him for a superb photo, and asked after the well-being of a fan who used to attend almost all his concerts. After establishing that personal connection, he started the performance with his popular song *Legend*. The song that released in February 2019 seemed to take on his adversaries directly, while declaring him a legend. In it he sings: '*Ho unlimited chalde ... baahar ni*.'

Unlimited is the enmity
Limited is the count of our breaths
I move opposite to the world
And parallel with death
In some hearts, I stay forever
And some others don't understand me

As the song ended, Moosewala addressed the crowd. 'People who are successful get so many enemies out of jealousy. But you [rivals or critics] can only bark like a dog later. The one who had to do something, achieve something, has done it. Now you can keep boasting you will do this or that but nothing is going to happen. You cannot do anything. The entire world knows who has stormed your world ... There is no need to tell them who has guts. They know it,' he said, with his trademark thigh thump.

'From my school days, I listened to songs by Black rappers and tried singing myself. I was among the first in the village to become an electrical engineer and later, I passed IELTS to go abroad. And now you will not clap because I am talking sense. If I had abused someone, you all would have cheered,' the singer sneered when the audience went quiet. 'No one wants to know about your personal sufferings. The audience wants tamasha, hyperbole and loud and open challenges to rivals,' Moosewala went on. After he had finished saying his piece, he proceeded to change the mood of the gathering.

He was, after all, a master performer who knew the pulse of his audience.

'I do not know who are the people who say that I am running a race to win. But they don't know that I am not a horse to run such races on unsure ground. This horse is destined to win the world. Our fight is not with Punjabi singers, but with foreigners. We are just one per cent of the world's singers. I will take Punjabis to the top slot.' That was it. The crowd cheered for him with gusto once again.

Calling himself a legend, Sidhu Moosewala bragged, 'So many people search for my house that Google has put a pin on the map. Fans come to my house as if it is their own. I also meet them as my family members and not fans. I never say no to anyone. And Google also shows my old house. The other singers don't tell fans where they live. They hide behind guards in cities. And I live openly for all of you,' he finished to loud screams and cheers.

After his killing, Google Maps added a new pin on the village of Moosa—Sidhu Moosewala's Memorial.

***

Ajay Pal Singh Brar has an interesting take on the massive fanbase of Moosewala.

He says that Moosewala showed a 'big-other' enemy in his songs, a stand-in almost for an existential crisis. 'You create an enemy, real or imaginary. The enemy's rise is a threat to your survival. When you see Moosewala's videos, you imagine your own big-other enemies.'

According to Brar, Moosewala didn't stop there. 'After creating the big-other enemy, he defeats him. And so do you in your imagination. That is how you are drawn to Moosewala.'

Brar says it is wrong to attribute gangsterism to singers like Moosewala. Gangster culture has always been a part of Punjab and is not something that was started by Moosewala. The Malwa region has a history of producing people who would be gangsters by today's standards but were then known as rebels or Robin Hoods who robbed from the rich and gave to the poor.

'Be it Bambiha, Shera Khuban, Lawrence Bishnoi, Jaipal Bhullar, Jaswinder Rocky or the father of this generation of gangsters, Dimpy Chandbhan, all and many more have emerged from this region,' says Brar. It is important to remember, according to Brar, that none of them went into a life of crime and extortion for money. 'It was a statement, that they existed. That they were something. It was just about making a name for themselves. In folklore, we hear the story of three brothers from the village of Jindwala in the pre-Independence era. They owned 5,000 acres of land and studied in a school run by the British. Still, they looted a bank. When asked in a court, they said they did it just for the thrill of it.'

Brar may not be too far off the mark. Dimpy Chandbhan had 150 acres of land and still he murdered people and formed a gang. At his wedding in the 1990s,

Uttar Pradesh gangster Mohd Ansari was a special guest. Dimpy had brought about the corporatisation of the gangs in the region.

Like the Scottish folk of old times, people in the Majha region indulged in lifting cattle. And at one time, people gave their daughter in marriage to a man who could prove he was strong enough to steal cattle. Resorting to crime as a show of strength is not new in Punjab. Hypermasculinity has always been the norm.

The criticism against Moosewala's glamourising of gun culture may not be unfounded but he was possibly part of a larger issue. As JNU scholars Harinder Happy and Shivam Mogha wrote, 'It is vital to acknowledge that Sidhu's references to weapons cannot be an excuse to let the state government evade responsibility for the gun culture in the state. After all, this culture has systematically been developed under political patronage over the past decades.'[9]

In the interview with Harjinder Thind for Red FM Canada, Moosewala spoke from his heart. 'Singing was my hobby. I don't know when it became a profession. Singing gave me satisfaction. People in their free time play or read or anything else. I sing. It is for my heart's contentment. Most of the songs are sung for money … I cannot respond to all my critics and those questioning me. So, I speak, I express through my song. These are not just lyrics of the song. These are my responses to the comments my critics leave on YouTube and other places,' he said and sang in the radio programme: '*Ho baapu mera ... thale rakhe dunia.*'

> My father advised me not to bother
> These people are true to none
> If a man has passion in his blood
> He can win over anything
> I support everyone with my heart
> Not hatch conspiracies
> The Almighty shelters me
> I keep the world under my shoes

Moosewala also spoke about the numbers game in the music industry and the fickleness of being on top. 'No one can be on top all the time. I replaced someone and someone will replace me. There is no nest in the sky. You will have to come to the ground. But as long as it is my time to shine, I will sing what I want and will sing the opposite of what some people want.'

'Listen to the Bambiha song. The slap Moosewala talks about was meant for us,' Lawrence had told H.G.S. Dhaliwal. Davinder Bambiha, when alive, had been Bishnoi's rival. The two had started their criminal operations around the same time. According to Bishnoi, the Bambiha song was Moosewala's eulogy to the kabaddi-player-turned-gangster.

But was it? Bains disagrees.

'This is not the first time that Bambiha, as a word, has been featured in a song. Though the videos clearly show the Bambiha character as a gangster in the Amrit Mann/ Moosewala song, the word has a different history,' he said.

Bambiha or papiha is a bird known for its sweet voice in Punjab. Due to the shape of the beak, the bird cannot drink water from a pond or a vessel like others. It cranes its neck towards the sky and prays for rain as it can only quench its thirst when rainwater drops into its open beak.

Bains's argument was that 'bambiha' or 'babiha' or 'papiha' were commonly used as metaphors for the soul's love for god, quite like the bird's longing for rain drops. The bird makes many appearances in folksongs as the harbinger of monsoon. The word 'bambiha' also means the beginning of wedding rituals in a family, when the nanke (maternal grandparents of the bride) bring a decorated bamboo plate for the bride as a ceremonious beginning of the wedding celebrations and preparations.

The bambiha bird even finds a mention in the Gurbani:

> *Baabeehaa khin khin bil-laai.*
> *Bin pir dekhe neend na paai.*
> (Guru Amar Das, Guru Granth Sahib, 1262)

The pied cuckoo cries out (for a drop of rain) each and every moment. It cannot sleep without seeing its beloved, the raincloud.[10]

Could Moosewala's 'Bambiha' have been about the cuckoo and the lesson of divinity it held within?

The police investigation seems to have started with Lawrence Bishnoi's animosity towards Sidhu Moosewala and ended with it. It is repeatedly said that Lawrence was upset with Moosewala for his alleged proximity to the Davinder Bambiha-Lucky Patial gang, who were Bishnoi's rivals. The murder of student-leader-turned-politician Vicky Middukhera is also supposed to have been a big provocation. But are these the only reasons?

Dr Nahar Singh, an award-winning Punjabi folklorist, critic and academician, who has written several books on Punjabi music and songs, has discussed songs on gangsters and violence in an interview with Kulvir Gojra on his YouTube channel, SukhanLok.[11] He terms the songs as detrimental to Punjabi folk history and literature. 'These songs, when referring to gang wars, appeal to your machismo and casteism. They are not intellectual. It is because of the popularity of such songs that, in Punjab, ghazal singing, Sufi music and literary lyrics have not thrived. Popular singing gets many followers and the big question is not just who is singing or writing these songs but mainly who is responding to them. And who forms the market for such songs?'

Promod Kumar, Director, Institute for Development and Communication (IDC), terms all the macho posturing or singing about the issues of Punjab as sheer economics or commercial exploitation. 'Punjab's dreamless youth run after desires without a strong ideology. And desires are vices. Moosewala's lyrics do not reflect Bhagat Singh or writer Pash's ambitions or dreams for the motherland. Their revolution had a direction, a destiny which rebellion alone may not have. In Moosewala's case, it seems only market logic is applied,' he said.

Sidhu Moosewala was a child of controversy. *295* created enough brouhaha, but its chutzpah appealed to the Punjabi spirit, known for its rebellious streak, unafraid of dissent. His songs are reminiscent of Dulla Bhatti, popularly referred to as the Robin Hood of Punjab in the fifteenth century. He was a famous Punjabi freedom fighter who, as folklore has it, led a revolt against the Mughals during Akbar's rule. In *295* Moosewala sings that freedom of speech is a mirage, and that no matter what you say publicly, controversy is inevitable. Notably, he had been booked twice under 294 IPC for 'Obscene acts and songs'.

Section 295 IPC deals with sacrilege, an issue that has changed the politics of Punjab in recent years. Moosewala sings in *295*: '*Museebat tan marda … hate milugi.*'

> Real men face trouble
> But don't feel the pressure
> Don't let the world enjoy your distress

On the path that you are walking on
You will get a high rate of infamy
And court daily controversy
You will get debates in the name of religion
Telling the truth will get you 295
Success will get you hate

Amit Bamzai wrote about the significance of this song. 'In the middle of the summer of year 2021, came a single from "Moosetape" that perhaps would be the most heard song by Moosewala. It is markedly different from the other blockbuster songs by the late artist in its theme and its depth. "295" became the anthem for the Punjabi community living in India and abroad with more than 260 million hits in less than 10 months of its launch. Its painful stanza depicting a sensitive relationship between a child and his father who reminds him of his unwavering support and the pride he took in his achievements was played all over the reels on Instagram when Balkaur Singh, Sidhu Moosewala's father, thanked all the fans that turned up on Sidhu's funeral.'[12]

Despite what his critics say, Moosewala did transform from a gun-toting, fast car-driving youth into a perceptive man infusing his songs with thought-provoking political commentary. In *Moosetape*, Moosewala conveyed a message to the youth to love their parents; his attempt to inculcate family values among his listeners amid concerns that families were drifting apart. Through the life he lived, he became an ambassador for the youth, encouraging them to stick to their roots. He returned to his native village and refused lucrative offers to move to Mumbai to work in the film industry. His life became a subtle message to the youth of Punjab, known for immigrating to foreign lands in search of greener pastures. He became a voice against this exodus. Who knows what direction his music would have taken had his life not been cut short?

FIFTEEN

DISPUTES

In 2014, an audio clip of a Punjabi film and music artist talking to a gangster over an internet phone was circulated online.

Actor (*pleading*): Please give me some time.

Gangster: We have already given you enough time. You listen now. Pay up immediately, otherwise your family will mourn forever.

Actor: I am trying, but sales are—

Gangster: Last time, you said you would call back. Now tell us plainly if you want to settle this or not. Killing you will make an example of you, and we will make money from thirty others. You will be like a dead crow hanging from a pole as a lesson to other crows. Don't show me your starry arrogance. If I show mine, you and your family will regret it.

Actor: Nahi, Veer ji ... please listen ... I was saying business is terrible. Give me time. I will call you back on this number.

Gangster: You have already seen that approaching the police won't benefit you. You gave my previous number to the police and I got some calls. But has it made a difference? Only I can protect you, and I can destroy you as well within seconds, wherever you may hide.

Actor: I plead with you, brother, please. This is the ninth such call I have received this year. How many people can I pay?

Gangster: You don't worry about anyone else. Tell the other callers my name and they will piss in their pants. You know very well how many are already under my protection. Call me in ten minutes and I will tell you how my men will collect the money.

The call disconnects.

The call transcript signals a new trend that emerged around 2013 in Pollywood, a term for the Punjabi film and music industry. The threat of gangsters, quite like that of the Mumbai mafia in the 1990s, had arrived in Punjab. The timing coincided with the spread of the drug menace in Punjab. It is believed that returns from drug smuggling had found a way to Pollywood indirectly. Drug use is common in Punjab. Previously, substance abusers mostly consumed opium or poppy husk, but the number was not alarming and the practice was considered normal, much like consuming liquor. But in the last two decades, chitta has taken over as the main drug along with other synthetic and psychotropic substances. These drugs originate from Afghanistan and reach Punjab via Pakistan and Kashmir.

Professor Gurbhajan Gill, former head of the Punjabi Sahit Akademi, and an expert on Punjabi culture, traditions and literature, points out in an article in the *Tribune* that in folk literature, songs and movies, there would always be a character who was an opium addict (amli) and the comic relief.[1] The sardar who enjoys his food and drink is also a common feature in the popularly sung *boliyan* (couplets) and *tappe* (folk songs characterised by their quick and rhythmic beat).

> *Khaan bakre te peen sharaba*
> *Putt Sardara dey*

> Eating meat and drinking daily
> Those are the sons of sardars

> or

> *Ucheya tibeya*
> *Ch daaru pee ke*
> *Botalan dabiya*

> On the high mound
> We drink as well as
> Bury bottles for safekeeping

So common was the consumption of opium that the British, in 1930, introduced provisions for licenced opium addicts to check the spread of the drug and discourage its abuse. The licenced addicts were given a specific dose of opium prescribed by doctors. At the time of Independence, Punjab had approximately 200 such addicts, but after 1983, no new licence have been issued. Now, the number is less than ten.

Opium and poppy husk have been considered happy drugs that make you work more—a boon for farmers and labourers in Punjab. It is also common knowledge that labourers from Bihar and Uttar Pradesh were secretly given these drugs to make them work longer in the fields during the Green Revolution, a practice that may still be continuing. Though the cultivation of opium—the milk of the poppy—is banned in Punjab, it is allowed in Rajasthan, Madhya Pradesh and Chhattisgarh, where the warm climate and low rainfall along with sandy, loamy soil is conducive to the cultivation of the crop. It is mandatory to deposit all produce—poppy husk, opium and edible seeds—with the central government, but there is regular pilferage.[2] Punjab's Fazilka and Bathinda districts share a border with Rajasthan, where poppy is cultivated. The states have a marked boundary, but unlike the international border, it is not sealed with barbed wire, as the states are not inimical to each other. The police of both states try to maintain vigil via patrols, CCTVs and police *nakkas* on roads, but it is practically impossible to guard nearly 90 km of border territory between them. Drugs are smuggled through without much difficulty.

In a 2017 report, the Observer Research Foundation called Punjab a transit point for drug smuggling.[3] India is sandwiched between the 'golden triangle' of drug trade—Vietnam, Myanmar and Thailand—and the 'golden crescent' of Iran, Afghanistan and Pakistan, where opium is produced. The golden crescent turned to Punjab for the transit of drugs from Afghanistan after China and Japan separately cracked down on the earlier routes. By 2013, Punjab recorded the highest number of drug related cases in the country, a trend which continues to date.[4] The state continues to rank among the top three in the country for the highest number of drug cases recorded under the Narcotics and Pyschotropic Substances (NDPS) Act. The extent of the addiction can be gauged from the fact that 3.3 lakh addicts were registered for de-addiction in the last six months of 2014.[5]

Over time, the drug menace has assumed alarming proportions. By April 2023, two governments, the SAD–BJP alliance and later, the Congress, were removed from power because of public anger at their failure to check the drug menace, among other issues. An Akali Dal minister was booked and arrested for facilitating international drug smuggling. Additional Inspector General of Police Raj Jit Singh was booked under the NDPS Act and dismissed from service.[6] The main accusation against him was that he had protected and promoted Inderjit Singh, an officer who had been dismissed for having dealings with substance abuse.

⁂

The Punjabi film and music industry also happened to grow exponentially around 2013. Dr Simran Sidhu of Doaba College, Jalandhar, writes about it in the *Global Media Journal*,[7] explaining that the period between the late 1970s and the mid-1990s were difficult not just in terms of political, social and economic development, but also the cultural development of the state. She writes that after the death of Varinder Singh, the superstar of Punjabi cinema, in 1988, the film industry faced a major setback and audiences, who had already avoided cinema halls because of the fear of terrorism, were completely disenchanted.

According to Dr Sidhu, things slowly started to improve in 2003 when *Jee Aayan Nu* released and infused some much-needed vigour into the film industry. But the real turnaround came in 2012 when twenty-four Punjabi movies were released. In 2013, the number had doubled to forty-two. The Punjabi film industry became a lucrative part of the Indian film business, with sixty-one Punjabi films releasing worldwide in 2019.

As the Punjabi film industry began to grow, the need for actors who would headline the films grew as well. Barring Jimmy Shergill, who had made a name for himself in mainstream Hindi films, there weren't too many actors who carried enough star power in Punjabi cinema. Punjabi singers such as Jasbir Jassi and Harbhajan Mann filled that gap instead, doubling up as actors.[8]

The subsequent years clearly established the growing influence of Punjabi singers in the film industry. The rise of singers-turned-actors, including Diljit Dosanjh, Gippy Grewal and Parmeesh Verma, underlined a golden formula for success—the combination of singing and acting worked to increase your star power. It was during these years that Sidhu Moosewala began working on establishing himself as a musician of a new creed—Punjab rap. But as the industry became more glamorous and lucrative, it also started attracting the attention of disruptive elements. Police officials and several insiders in Pollywood privately admit that the growth of the Punjabi film industry has been directly proportional to the rise of criminal activity, drug smuggling and addiction in Punjab. It is believed that returns from the drug trade found their way into the film and music industries.

In February 2017, the Anti-Narcotics Cell (ANC) of the Mumbai Police nabbed a Punjabi film producer for using drug money to finance two Punjabi films.[9] He had allegedly supplied 5 kg mephedrone (also known as meow meow), worth around Rs 1.5 crore, to a gang that dealt in drugs in Mumbai. In February 2020, a Punjabi film actor and some producers were held in connection with a haul of 450 kg heroin from a port in Gujarat. The Enforcement Directorate of India, which is mandated to probe money laundering and illegal financial transactions, asserted that the accused had pumped money into the Punjabi film and music industries.[10] Several such isolated cases have been reported since 2014.

Apparently, rampant drug smuggling enjoys political and police protection. Between 2014 and 2017, over a hundred police officers in Punjab were arrested and dismissed from service for helping smugglers.[11] Patronage of smugglers by politicians, especially the SAD, was a political issue in the 2017 and 2022 Assembly elections, as well as the 2014 and 2019 Lok Sabha elections.[12]

The music industry in Punjab has over 450 registered music labels that release around twenty to twenty-five songs every day. In 2021, the industry released over 5,000 music videos. Promod Kushwaha, DCP (Special Cell), New Delhi, has stressed on the link between gangsters and the Punjabi film and music industries. 'Extortion and protection money is now an accepted practice with the underworld gangs aiming to gain a share in it. The culture of violence has also become an integral part of Punjabi music with more and more young rappers normalising violence through their genre of gangster rap,' Kushwaha said.[13]

Police officials have acknowledged that the increasing number of cases of extortion and violence are due to the proximity between the stars and the underworld. The nexus is effective because the music industry is an easy source of 'white' money for gangsters. In exchange for the copyright of a song or two, gangsters offer their protection to artists. However, it is a dangerous alliance that often sours.

Since the involvement with gangs often begins at the college level for students in Punjab, gang members are sometimes fans of the singers and initially help them get their payments on time from producers.

Vikram Mehra, the managing director of Saregama and the current chairman of the trade body of the Indian music industry which represents the interests of over 200 music labels across the country, was quoted as saying, 'The current monetary value of India's music industry is Rs 1,300 crore out of which the annual turnover of the Punjabi music industry is around Rs 200 crore with an additional Rs 500 crore coming from live shows. Thus, Punjabi music has the largest share of approximately Rs 700 crore in the independent music industry of India, which is almost five times the size of the Telugu music industry, the second-largest market in the category.'[14]

Senior journalist Sanjeev K. Jha wrote in *Hindustan Times* that, as per an Intelligence Bureau (IB) officer working in Punjab, there is a possibility of involvement of black money in the music industry.

'The influx of black money makes it lucrative for gangsters to give extortion calls to artistes and producers. Several music companies, such as Thug Life and Gold Media (these two were unearthed during the crackdown by the Punjab Police), are being directly run by gangsters abroad. The gangsters have been investing extortion money in these music companies,' the IB officer said.[15]

The music labels Thug Life and Gold Media feature in another police investigation. In August 2021, the Mohali police captured three persons for attacking Parmeesh Verma and threatening the actor-singer Gippy Grewal. The three belonged to the Davinder Bambiha gang, run by his aides Lucky Patial (who is based abroad) and Sukhpreet Budha (in a jail cell in Punjab). Mohali SSP Satinder Singh stated, 'The [Bambiha] gang has been involved in extorting money from industrialists after threatening them on phone. It has further invested the money in two music companies: Thug Life and Gold Media.'

It was amid this unholy nexus of drugs, money and the influence of the gangsters in Pollywood that Sidhu Moosewala set out to spread his wings.

The same controversial music labels—Thug Life and Gold Media—would also have a bearing on his career. The rapper, as investigations after his death revealed, had been caught in the tug of war between gang members killing each other for control of Pollywood.

Many who knew him say that Moosewala transformed after he migrated to Canada to pursue his dollar dreams like several Punjabi youth. For them, Canada offers greener pastures and a free life uncontrolled by parents. Late-night parties, official dates and live-in relationships are still taboo for most young Indians growing up outside the metros. As per the records of the Punjab government, on an average, one lakh youth migrate abroad every year. For many, the lack of employment opportunities in Punjab is a major factor for the move. In February 2020, Christopher Kerr, Director, Operations for Immigration, Refugees and Citizenship Canada (IRCC), said there was about a 400 per cent increase in Indian youth migrating to Canada over the past few years. Punjab constitutes nearly 60 per cent of that number.[16]

Shubhdeep was one of many such youngsters who moved to Canada for a better life. He settled in Brampton and registered for an advanced course in engineering to become eligible for employment in Canada. Punjabis constitute 2.3 per cent of the population in Canada and most of them live in Surrey or Brampton.

As per the police investigation after his murder, interviews with his parents and friends, reports in the media and videos on YouTube, Moosewala found his calling as a rap artist and performer in Brampton's disco and music clubs. He had already begun writing songs during his college days in Ludhiana. Now he started writing more and performing them.

His first song, *License*, became a hit and he began to be spoken of as a new lyricist to watch out for. As he gained popularity, he became friends with prominent artists like Deep Jandu, Elly Mangat, Sunny Malton, Byg Byrd and Karan Aujla.

By the next year, his popularity had grown even more. Some of his enterprising friends in Brampton, who had formed a group called the Bandook Group, decided to form a music company. They called it Thirteen Music Records. In February 2017, Moosewala sang *G-Wagon*, which was released by the record label Humble Music, owned by actor-singer Gippy Grewal. It was a hit and was followed by an even bigger hit, *So High*, which catapulted Moosewala to celebrity status. He bagged the best lyricist award for *So High* at the Brit Asia TV Music Awards in 2017.[17]

Sidhu Moosewala had arrived.

However, despite the accolades and growing fame, Sidhu and his friends did not know much about sales and marketing and failed to make profits. They needed professional help. This was when Kanwarpal Grewal, who was from Ludhiana and had settled in Brampton, approached him. He was a member of a group called Brampton Wale Ladke (The Brampton Boys), which was associated with the Bandook Group.

He roped in Jyoti Pandher, and the two formed a music label, Jatt Life Records, and took over Moosewala's songs. The Bandook Group did not like the fact that a new record label would now be controlling Sidhu's music. Things escalated and a bloody brawl broke out in a bar in Brampton between Kanwar and others. It led to a police case against both groups. Sidhu Moosewala was not present on the scene when the brawl took place.

As per the agreement with Jatt Life, Moosewala would get 30 per cent of the returns from his music. The group launched several songs, including his first album, *PBX1*, in October 2018. The album made nearly Rs 2 crore, but Sidhu, after paying off the expenses incurred on foreign tours, made only about Rs 30 lakh. The same year, he released the highly popular *Jatt da Muqabala*, which shook the music charts worldwide.

Moosewala was invited to concerts worldwide. But in terms of money, he was still not making much.

Wiser with experience, Moosewala realised that if he wanted to keep the maximum share of the profits, he would have to launch his own label. He broke away from Grewal and the others and his eponymous record label, Sidhu Moosewala, was born. However, Jatt Life Records wouldn't let go of their golden goose that easily. They released some songs and made copyright claims on titles released by Sidhu independently. By this time, Moosewala had returned to his village. He was far from being the darling of the police or the government, who accused him of encouraging gun culture. Call it the non-cooperation of the Mansa district police or the influence of Jatt Life Records, but Moosewala could not get a police complaint registered against his previous record label. His music label had started doing well, but he faced harassment through infringement of copyright and claimed he was being threatened as well. He was given examples of singers who had suffered after disputes with music label companies over copyright and infringement of agreements.

In February 2020, Moosewala's father lodged an FIR in the Ropar police district against Kanwarpal Grewal for leaking Moosewala's song *El Chapo*. He alleged the leak cost Moosewala Rs 70 lakh. It was interesting that the FIR was lodged in Ropar district and not in Moosewala's home district of Mansa. The reigning Congress government under Captain Amarinder Singh was not very sympathetic towards Moosewala because of his songs, videos and lifestyle. The complaint could only be filed with the help of a friendly cop from Ropar.

⎯⎯∞⎯⎯

After taking responsibility for Moosewala's murder, Goldy Brar, in an interview with senior journalist Ritesh Lakhi on the latter's YouTube channel, mentioned the music labels Thug Life and Gold Media, and a man called Arshdeep who was running the labels. Arshdeep was later caught by the Mohali police in an extortion racket run by gangsters. Police banned the music labels as well. As per the police investigation, Thug Life and Gold Media had the backing of gangsters Lucky Patial and Sukhpreet Budha.

Before being banned, the music labels released a song by a new singer, which featured Sidhu Moosewala. According to the police, as well as some singers, this was the music labels' way of telling the world that Sidhu Moosewala was under their protection. Police officials also claim that an associate of the gangsters, a former student leader at Panjab University, actively campaigned for Moosewala when the singer was contesting the Punjab Assembly elections from Mansa. But Moosewala had never confirmed or suggested that he had sought the backing of these gangsters. And now, with him gone, the truth will forever be obscured.

SIXTEEN

THE WAIT FOR JUSTICE

31 OCTOBER 2022

Balkaur Singh had not aged as much in all fifty-seven years of his life as he has since his son's monstrous killing on 29 May 2022.

His robust body has shrivelled and he looks like a shadow of his previous self. The pain his eyes reflect is not just on account of losing a young son, but also the wait for justice.

Much, however, has happened since. Police nabbed two shooters, Priyavrat and Kashish, on 20 June and the third, Ankit Sersa, on 2 July. Of the remaining three, the two Punjabi shooters Jagroop Roopa and Mannu Kusa were killed in an encounter with the Punjab Police in Tarn Taran on 22 July. Balkaur was called to identify the shooters. He saw the two bodies and told the media, 'This is what happens when you kill someone. But this is not the end. There will be more funeral pyres. There are more accused involved in my son's killing roaming out there free. These were just pawns.'

The sixth, Deepak Mundi, was the last person to be arrested among the shooters. On 11 September, police authorities from Delhi and Punjab, with the help of Central agencies, arrested him close to the Nepali border on the Indian side. He had managed to evade arrest for three months and thirteen days.

On 17 October, the Punjab Police arrested two persons, Avtar and Jagtar, who were Moosewala's neighbours.[1] Their house was across the road, in an agricultural field, opposite the singer's haveli. In a supplementary complaint to the police, Balkaur had alleged that CCTV cameras installed on Avtar's and Jagtar's properties were aimed at his haveli. It was suspected that the accused gangsters could have kept an eye on the movement outside the haveli through these cameras.

But the biggest shock was still to come.

Each police district in a state has several police stations with their specific area of jurisdiction. Each police station is headed by a Station House Officer (SHO). The SHOs do not have jurisdiction in each other's areas, but that is where the Crime Investigation Agency (CIA) comes in. The CIA has jurisdiction in all the districts and carries out major operations and investigations. It is like a combination of the detective and homicide squads in Western countries. The primary role of the CIA wing is the prevention or resolution of criminal activity. The in-charge of the CIA wing is usually someone with the rank of inspector or, in some cases, a sub-inspector. The in-charge is usually handpicked by the district police chief or the senior superintendent of police.

In Mansa, the CIA in-charge at the time of Moosewala's murder was Inspector Pritpal Singh. The CIA is supposed to keep an eye on suspicious elements and in Moosewala's case, several modules of gang members had been surveying the village and the area around his house. Considering that Moosewala had been under police protection, it is worth noting that neither the CIA in-charge nor the SSP or SHO of the district were transferred after his murder.

It doesn't end there. During the investigation, the Mansa police transferred a Haryana gangster named Deepak Tinu from Tihar Jail and named him in the Moosewala murder case. In the police challan, Tinu is accused of providing logistical support to the shooters in the case. He is said to be very close to Lawrence Bishnoi and to have a network in the country and abroad. He was sent to the jail in Goindwal. On 27 September, the CIA brought him back for questioning in a murder case.

On the night of 1 October, he escaped from the custody of the Mansa CIA.[2] Sub Inspector Pritpal Singh was arrested the next morning on the basis of allegations that he had taken Tinu to his residence where they had alcohol.[3] Tinu's girlfriend Jatinder Kaur also reached Pritpal's house. According to the police, the inspector left them alone in his bedroom and dozed off in the other room. Tinu and his girlfriend escaped. It took the police ten days to nab her. After being caught in Mumbai, she told the police that Tinu had escaped to the Maldives.

Yet again, it was the Delhi Police that succeeded in arresting Deepak Tinu. In an operation led by H.G.S. Dhaliwal, Tinu was traced and arrested in Ajmer, Rajasthan on 19 October.

But that was still not the end of the embarrassment for the Punjab Police. Chandigarh/Mohali police arrested someone called Mohit Aggarwal, who, in his interrogation, revealed that he had taken Inspector Pritpal Singh for shopping in Chandigarh several times and had arranged for his stay in a hotel where girls were also supplied. As per news reports, this happened in the month of July. At that time, the shooters Roopa and Mannu Kusa were on the run and Deepak Mundi had not yet been arrested.

In a media conference held after the revelations made by Mohit, Balkaur asked, 'What is the meaning of a Punjab police officer wining and dining members of the Lawrence Bishnoi gang? Why were they taking him out for shopping? And pleasure trips?'

'The government is providing all facilities inside jails, there is no hope of justice. We will carry out candle marches across state. Where is the badlav (change)?' Charan lamented.

'I am not saying the inspector is involved in my son's killing, but he was busy with activities other than his job of preventing crime. Those who were involved in the physical assault, in the killing of my son, have been arrested but the masterminds—and these are not the gangsters—are yet to be identified. I regret to announce that I will soon leave the country with my wife as we don't have hope for justice here,' Balkaur said.

SEVENTEEN

ALL THAT IS LEFT BEHIND

1 MAY 2023

In the past, Balkaur had a simple routine: as he woke up every morning, his feet would automatically take him to his son's room. He never failed to check on him first thing, every day. Sidhu Moosewala used to be a late riser. He would work on his songs through the stillness of the night and wake up much after the sun had risen.

Since Sidhu's death in May 2022, Balkaur has a new morning ritual: to get up and go to his son's Thar. Like his son, the car had also been embedded with several bullets. Balkaur cleans it gently, as if nursing his son's wounds.

He has not replaced the Thar's bullet-ridden windshield. It serves as a reminder to the police and the government that the wounds are open; that as far as he is concerned, the real killers are still at large.

After tending to the car, Balkaur walks to Sidhu Moosewala's statue, some 400 m away from the village across the Mansa-Talwandi Sabo road.

These days, however, Balkaur has to gather all his strength just to get out of bed. In January, he underwent an angioplasty for the second time since the 'butchers' killed his son. Doctors cleared his arteries and inserted a stent.

'The doctors said the stent would improve blood flow and prevent fat accumulation. But can it filter the sorrow and sighs my heart pumps every moment? Can my heart ever beat normally again?' Balkaur asks his wife. Charan, who has brought him tea, places the cup on the bedside table and moves swiftly to his side to help him up.

'*Tussi kahal na karo. Doctor ne holi holi uthan nu keha*,' she says. (Don't get up so quickly. Doctors have asked you to do it slowly.)

'I want to be able to meet the public today. We have missed a few Sundays,' Balkaur tells her. He takes a few paces before sitting down again and taking a small sip of his tea. On almost every Sunday since cruel destiny snatched away their only son, the couple has opened the doors of their haveli for visitors, who are mostly fans of the singer.

'You take it easy,' Charan whispers, rubbing his back gently. 'I only have you now. You should rest till you regain your strength. This is a long fight. But we have to keep it going.' She sits rigidly, controlling her sobs.

Not a day has passed since the death of their son when the couple has not cried out for justice. Balkaur met Punjab DGP Gaurav Yadav a couple of times concerning allegations that some singers and music producers had also been behind the conspiracy to eliminate his son. 'The gangsters are just a tool in the hands of these musicians. But none have been caught,' Balkaur had said in the complaint to the police. He reiterated the same to the National Investigation Agency (NIA), the premier anti-terror investigation taskforce in India. Among other things, the NIA investigates terror funds routed to India through kabaddi matches, music shows and films. While the NIA has questioned several Punjabi singers and music producers on their alleged links with gangsters, no one has been arrested.[1] Moreover, the agency has not officially taken up the Moosewala case.

On 1 September 2022, media reports said Anmol Bishnoi and Sachin Thapan Bishnoi, the younger brother and nephew of Lawrence Bishnoi, who were also among the top accused in Moosewala's killing, had been detained in Kenya and Azerbaijan respectively.[2] Sachin and Anmol had allegedly helped the shooters with logistical support. How had the two suspects managed to leave India? No one had any answers. Police said they had used fake passports, but was it really that simple for suspects in a murder case to flee on the basis of fake documents, if they didn't have someone helping them? The questions continue to haunt Balkaur.

More shocking news was to follow. On 19 April 2023, Anmol Bishnoi was spotted dancing at a wedding in California. Performing at the same wedding were Punjabi singers Karan Aujla and Sherry Mann.[3] The video of Anmol, who was supposed to be in detention in Kenya, went viral. 'How could he reach the US if he was detained and what was he doing at the event featuring Karan Aujla, with whom my son had a well-known tiff?' Balkaur said in a video.[4] 'This is heart-breaking for a common man, a father like me. Everyone else but us—my wife and I—seem to have the resources to do anything.'

Karan Aujla issued a statement later disassociating himself from the controversy. He said that both he and Sherry Mann had been booked to perform at the wedding. He had no idea who the guests at the wedding were. In fact, he stressed, he was not even aware of the 'questionable individual' who was seen dancing at his show, till he saw the social media posts about the incident.

In March 2023, Balkaur was preparing to celebrate his son's death anniversary. 'The first death anniversary is observed after ten months in our culture instead of twelve. So, we announced a big programme and expected lakhs of people, dignitaries, political leaders, actors and musicians to attend. The state government tried convincing us for a smaller programme, fearing law and order problems. I told them to first catch the real killers, and also those who had leaked my son's security withdrawal detail to the media,' said Balkaur.

Then, on 14 March, the Lawrence Bishnoi interview appeared with Jagwinder Patial of ABP News.[5] Apparently, the interview was done via phone, since Lawrence was in the high-security Bathinda prison, only 60 km from Moosewala's house. In the video that was telecast, Lawrence had a flowing beard and could be heard calmly presenting his point of view. He spoke in straightforward terms about his crimes and seemed to be unrepentant.

The government was left red-faced when the video was telecast. Questions rose about how the interview could have been conducted and with such clear sound and video quality. Especially since Lawrence was in a high-security jail, where purportedly no mobile network was available. Punjab DGP Gaurav Yadav and Additional Director General of Police (ADGP), Prisons B. Chandrashekhar called a press conference in Chandigarh and claimed Lawrence was not in Punjab when the interview was recorded. They said Lawrence had been shifted to Bathinda jail from a Rajasthan jail and implied that the interview could have been conducted in that jail. Also, the DGP reasoned, 'He doesn't have a yellow T-shirt with collar with him which he is wearing in the interview. And he is sporting a flowing beard. Whereas he had trimmed his beard when he was taken from the Rajasthan jail by our team.' The DGP released his latest photos, showing him in an orange shirt without a collar, with his beard trimmed.

On 17 March, another interview of Lawrence with the same journalist was aired on the same channel. This time, he was wearing exactly the same clothes, as seen in the photos released by the Punjab DGP. The interview was a direct challenge to the Punjab Police. An inquiry was ordered on how the interview was conducted. In fact, in the video Lawrence is heard saying that everything is possible in jail. 'There are some loopholes in the security which we use,' he admitted, laughing.[6]

Balkaur felt that the interview and its timing were deliberate. The motive, he believed, was to tarnish Sidhu's image.

It is interesting that a prominent media channel had access to Lawrence for a phone interview. But why interview only Lawrence Bishnoi? There were several other gangsters in jails in Punjab. No one has ever interviewed the rival Bambiha gang members, who are also lodged in Punjab jails. Why was Lawrence given the chance to put his point across?

Coincidentally, a day before Sidhu Moosewala's death anniversary, the Punjab Police launched a massive crackdown on Khalistani ideologue Amritpal Singh. The entire state was sealed and internet services were suspended. More than 200 people, including eight core members of Amritpal's team, were arrested, but Amritpal managed to escape. A side-effect of the police crackdown and the suspension of internet services was that many could not reach the village of Moosa for Moosewala's death anniversary. Balkaur lamented that he could not even stream the tribute paid to his son live for his followers.

⸙

As the month of May approaches, more and more fans start trickling in to pay their respects to their hero and his parents.

Balkaur and Charan prepare themselves for a day of meeting fans and mourners. Outside the haveli, people gather for a darshan of the parents and to take a closer look at their beloved singer's house. The crowd includes friends, relatives, villagers and several ardent followers who keep visiting to offer their condolences, show solidarity, bow before Moosewala's statue and click selfies. Several media teams also routinely wait outside the gates.

Among the crowd is Rukhsana from Anantnag in Kashmir. 'Moosewala is in our hearts. He sang for those whose voices are muzzled,' she says, humming couplets from *295*.

She can remember crying as she swayed to this song at Jashn-e-Kashmir, a cultural festival organised by the Indian security agencies and Punjabi singers near the Dal Lake to portray 'normalcy' in the war-torn Kashmir Valley.[7] According to Bunty Bains, the musical event became a Moosewala event in no time. 'The public wanted us to perform only his songs,' he says. 'And *295* was the most demanded song. It has a certain outcry that everyone, who feels their voice is muzzled, can relate to.'

Mony Yadav from Meerut and Sushil Kumar from Allahabad are also among the hundred or so visitors who have thronged to the haveli from different parts of the country. They first visit Moosewala's statue before making their way to the his house.

A group of four bikers from Haryana and two from Ganganagar in Rajasthan also visit the spot in the village of Jawaharke where the singer was shot. The bikers tell others the story of how Moosewala had been waylaid. A sheet of fibreglass covers the bullet marks on the wall of the puncture shop. The singer's followers take selfies and photos of the bullet marks circled in white and framed in glass. Several photos of Moosewala are also fixed on the wall.

In one, the singer is performing on stage, holding a mike in his left hand. His right hand is a fist, with the index finger pointing outwards. Another is a still from one of his videos.

'This is a shrine,' says Mony Yadav while the others nod. From one of the several stalls selling Moosewala merchandise, he has bought two T-shirts with Moosewala's photos printed on them. T-shirts, bandanas, posters, cups and anything on which they could paste his photo—the stalls have everything for sale.

Posters with Moosewala's face shining bright proclaim, 'Legends never die.'

Visitors must enter their names, addresses, phone numbers and vehicle numbers before they are allowed inside the haveli to meet Moosewala's parents.

Inside, there is another ring of guards. These are the Punjab Police commandos and members of the SOG, deployed for the security of the slain singer's parents.

One can't help but think that if the police had taken the threats to the singer's life seriously and provided appropriate security cover, he would probably have been still alive, releasing chart-topping numbers for his fans.

Rukhsana hugs Charan and bursts into tears. She howls as she hugs Balkaur. '*Bahut burra hua*,' she says, her voice hoarse. She clings to them as a close relative might. Balkaur gets many such hugs all day as he meets his son's followers. Overwhelmed fans take their pictures, talk to them and commiserate over their mutual loss.

'You all have been my real strength. And the reason for hope. The love you have given us keeps us going,' Balkaur says. The aged parents meet everyone with folded hands, accept hugs and gently tap the head and shoulders of those who cry ceaselessly.

Less than an hour later, Balkaur speaks with a newfound strength in his voice. The despondency and frailty of the morning seem forgotten as he appears energised by the hundred or so visitors.

'Nearly ten months have passed since the demons took away our beloved Shubhdeep. But still, the police have been unable to catch or even identify the real cuplrits responsible for the killing. Yes, they have Lawrence and others. But what about those who asked Lawrence to kill? I can't believe gangsters did this on their own. There are stronger powers behind it. As if to mock us, Chief Minister Bhagwant Mann has deputed forty guards from the Punjab Police for round-the-clock security of his wife.[8] When they reduced security coverage for my son, this same government, the same AAP leaders, their spokespersons and media handlers claimed they were ending the VIP culture in Punjab. In ten months, their definition of the VIP culture has changed,' says the aggrieved father.

'I will take to the streets for justice if the government fails to find out who gave the gangsters crores of rupees to kill my son. And to relive the moments of the last ride of my son, I will be riding the same vehicle, the Thar, which he drove. I have not replaced the broken windshield of the car after it was damaged in the attack. I will drive it without a roof on the same route, in the hope that the government will act against the real culprits. I will not rest till the killers meet their end like Roopa and Mannu or are hanged to death.'

The people around are moved by Balkaur's words and raise the Sikh jaikar, '*Jo bole so nihaal, Sat Sri Akal.*'

Balkaur calms down and mingles some more. In the middle of talking to this writer, he suddenly rises and tells his wife, 'I must go and look at the fields today. I wonder what condition the wheat is in. Shubh used to do this.'

He leaves, only to return in the evening. A team of landscape designers from New Delhi have arrived to meet the parents and show them different designs for Moosewala's memorial. 'It should be a peaceful place, something that soothes the eyes,' Charan says to the designers.

As the sun goes down and the clock strikes five, the couple cling to each other. At this time, every day, they can feel their hearts sink. For it was around this time on 29 May that their son left home, never to return.

NOTES

CHAPTER 1: THE LAST RIDE

1. 'On the day of the shooting, Kekda and Nikku video called Goldy', (https://www.indiatoday.in/india/story/sidhu-moose-wala-shot-dead-9th-attempt-bullet-proof-car-saved-him-1964706-2022-06-20)

2. 'Punjabi by Nature: Punjab's Game of Thrones', (https://www.hindustantimes.com/punjab/punjabi-by-nature-punjab-s-game-of-thrones/story-sMx8Hm SnOVDb3ALuwVQiAM.html).

3. The India Ahead video clip of Moosewala's video is available at https://www.youtube.com/watch?v=QoMnr-j2mwI (June 2022)

CHAPTER 2. NOT JUST A RAP STAR

1. 'Minister Bhagwant Mann announced minimum support price for moong dal', (https://indianexpress.com/article/cities/chandigarh/punjab-cm-bhagwant-mann-announces-msp-on-moong-dal-7903858/).

2. 'More than 200 farm unions from 22 states organise a nationwide road blockade': (https://qz.com/india/1920840/a-timeline-of-the-months-long-farmer-protests-in-india).

3. 'Three women farm protesters from Punjab killed, (https://www.hindustantimes.com/cities/chandigarh-news/3-women-farm-protesters-from-punjab-killed-as-truck-hits-them-in-bahadurgarh-101635396705294.html)

4. Moosewala's film *Moosa Jatt* is based on the farmers' protest against the proposed changes in the farm laws. The poster showed his iconic tractor, 5911. https://twitter.com/iSidhuMooseWala/status/ 1436527414843252737/photo/1

5. The CCTV footage of Moosewala's Thar, right before the murder, is available at https://www.youtube.com/watch?v=ba_DrahYZaY

6. '19 wounds found on Sidhu Moosewala's body: Report', (https://www.tribuneindia.com/news/punjab/19-wounds-found-on-body-report-400449)

CHAPTER 3. THE FATHER

1. 'He had more than 10 million subscribers', (https://www.hindustantimes.com/cities/chandigarh-news/singerpolitician-who-was-shrouded-in-controversy-101653854221963.html).

CHAPTER 4. THE THREATS

1. 'From juvenile labourer to gangster: life of Shahrukh, a suspect in the Moosewala murder', (https://www.hindustantimes.com/cities/delhi-news/from-juvenile-labourer-to-gangster-life-of-shahrukh-a-suspect-in-the-moosewala-murder-101654452040106.html).

2. '"Welcome to the fold champ," tweeted Punjab Congress President Navjot Singh Sidhu': https://www.thequint.com/news/politics/sidhu-moose-wala-joins-congress-who-is-he.

3. 'The state crime branch registered a fourth case against him', (https://timesofindia.indiatimes.com/city/ludhiana/despite-multiple-firs-moose-wala-evades-law/articleshow/77074744.cms)

4. The video of Sidhu Moosewala's interview is available at https://www.youtube.com/watch?v=JVb6PgIdjHE.

5. 'Dilpreet Singh will now be questioned for seeking protection money from Punjabi singer and actor Gippy Grewal, (https://www.hindustantimes.com/punjab/gangster-dilpreet-to-be-quizzed-for-threat-calls-to-punjabi-actor-gippy-grewal/story-qTAZ1a0K8duzMOic8GGX8M.html).

CHAPTER 5. LAWRENCE BISHNOI

1. The *India Today* video clip of Goldy Brar's confession tape is available at https://www.youtube.com/watch?v=YuSmlf8gTik (Jul 2022)

2. 'Witnesses turn hostile in poaching case against Salman Khan',(https://zeenews.india.com/news/nation/witnesses-turn-hostile-in-poaching-case-against-salman_43552.html).

3. 'Eyewitness's testimony and forensic reports helped nail Salman Khan in blackbuck poaching case', (https://www.indiatoday.in/mail-today/story/eyewitness-s-testimony-and-forensic-reports-helped-nail-salman-khan-in-blackbuck-poaching-case-1205913-2018-04-05.

4.   'Gangster Bishnoi Threatens to Kill Salman Khan in Jodhpur', (https://timesofindia.indiatimes.com/city/jaipur/gangster-bishnoi-threatens-to-kill-salman-in-jodhpur/articleshow/62387117.cms).

5.   'MCOCA against Lawrence Bishnoi … and nine others for running a crime syndicate', (https://timesofindia.indiatimes.com/city/delhi/gangster-aides-with-pan-india-plans-charged-under-mcoca/articleshow/86354696.cm).

CHAPTER 6. THE KILLERS

1.   The Punjab Opiod Dependence Survey, 2015, (http://web.stanford.edu/~rm89/Punjab_AIIMS_Report.pdf).

2.   'More than half of Punjab's prison inmates involved in drug cases', (https://theprint.in/india/more-than-half-of-punjabs-prison-inmates-involved-in-drugs-cases-says-jails-minister/273099/)

3.   'He fired at least six rounds from two pistols', (https://www.tribuneindia.com/news/punjab/sidhu-moosewala-killing-who-is-ankit-sirsa-described-by-cops-as-most-desperate-shooter-409476).

4.   'On the run for 105 days, sixth shooter caught', (https://www.tribuneindia.com/news/punjab/on-the-run-for-105-days-sixth-shooter-mundi-held-at-nepal-border-430485)

CHAPTER 7. CHAUHAN

1.   'Punjab Police: Too Many Wings Hampering Policing', (https://www.hindustantimes.com/cities/chandigarh-news/punjab-police-too-many-wings-hamper-policing-say-experts-101649274224103.html).

2. 'The man who shot dead Bishnoi's aide Gurlal Brar',
    (https://www.hindustantimes.com/cities/chandigarh-
    news/man-who-shot-dead-bishnoi-s-aide-gurlal-brar-in-
    chandigarh-arrested-101627155797395).

3. 'Gurlal's murder is an attack on our family': the interview
    can be seen at https://www.youtube.com/watch?v=VQ9g
    NfBLdlk.

4. 'Two shooters held in Faridkot Cong leader Gurlal Singh
    Pehalwan murder case', (https://www.tribuneindia.com/
    news/punjab/2-shooters-held-in-faridkot-cong-leader-
    gurlal-singh-pehalwan-murder-case-240532).

5. 'Youth Akali Dal leader Vikramjit Middukhera shot dead
    in Punjab's Mohali' , (https://www.indiatoday.in/india/
    story/youth-akali-dal-leader-vicky-middukhera-shot-
    dead-punjab-mohali-1838074-2021-08-07)

6. 'Dimpy murder case: Court acquits Jaswinder Singh',
    (https://indianexpress.com/article/cities/chandigarh/
    dimpy-murder-case-court-acquits-jaswinder-singh/).

CHAPTER 8. THE CATCHER

1. 'Wanted gangster Kala Rana in Ambala STF custody',
    (https://www.hindustantimes.com/cities/chandigarh-
    news/wanted-gangster-kala-rana-in-ambala-stf-
    custody-101648931734332.html).

2. 'Vicky Middukhera murder: Year on, real motive not known',
    (https://www.tribuneindia.com/news/punjab/middukhera-
    murder-year-on-real-motive-not-known-417511)

3. 'Jitender Gogi's courtroom murder planned months in
    advance', (https://indianexpress.com/article/cities/delhi/ rohini-
    courtroom-shootout-jitender-gogi-murder-7686100/).

CHAPTER 9. THE INVESTIGATION

1. 'Don't give custody to Punjab Police: Lawrence Bishnoi', (http://timesofindia.indiatimes.com/articleshow/91927079. cms?utm_source=contentofinterest&utm_medium= text&utm_campaign=cppst).
2. 'Fresh Complaint Filed Against Sidhu Moosewala For Hurting Religious Sentiments', (https://www. ghaintpunjab.com/ghaintpunjab/Article/31219/fresh-complaint-filed-against-sidhu-moosewala-for-hurting-religious-sentiments)
3. 'Sidhu Moosewala killing: Cops who cracked gangsters' network', (https://www.tribuneindia.com/news/punjab/ cops-who-cracked-gangsters-network-412433).
4. '60 gangsters, worldwide web of informers and gang rivalry is what it took to plan and execute Sidhu Moosewala's killing, shows police finding', (https://www.tribuneindia.com/news/ punjab/case-of-gang-rivalry-insist-cops-412153?ref=epaper).

CHAPTER 10. CATCHING THE SHOOTERS

1. 'Drug Addiction, Adverse Circumstances: The Stories Of Two Gangsters Killed In Sidhu Moosewala Case', (https:// www.outlookindia.com/national/drug-addiction-adverse-circumstances-the-stories-of-two-gangsters-killed-in-sidhu-moosewala-case-news-211181).
2. 'Sidhu Moose Wala murder case: Gangster's girlfriend led cops to killers of Punjabi pop singer', (https://www. timesnownews.com/mirror-now/in-focus/sidhu-moose-wala-murder-case-gangsters-girlfriend-led-cops-to-killers-of-punjabi-pop-singer-article-92359521#:~:text=It%20 is%20said%20his%20girlfriend,said%20Priyavrat%20 had%20three%20girlfriends).

CHAPTER 11: THE ENCOUNTER OF BONNIE AND CLYDE

1. 'Punjab ready with Special Operations Group to counter terror attacks', (https://www.hindustantimes.com/punjab/ punjab-ready-with-special-operations-group-to-counter-terror-attacks/story-vYERnlN72hZO2X4A22gPCP. html).

2. 'Sidhu Moosewala's killers Jagroop Rupa, Manpreet Manu killed after 4-hour encounter in Amritsar', (https:// www.tribuneindia.com/news/punjab/encounter-between-police-gangsters-on-in-amritsar-village-414094)

3. 'Drug Addiction, Adverse Circumstances: The Stories Of Two Gangsters Killed In Sidhu Moosewala Case', (https:// www.outlookindia.com/national/drug-addiction-adverse-circumstances-the-stories-of-two-gangsters-killed-in-sidhu-moosewala-case-news-211181).

CHAPTER 12. THE MOTHER

1. The interview with Sonam Bajwa can be seen on https:/ www.facebook.com/watch/?v=509348793754040

2. 'An emotional mother of Sidhu Moosewala at the Bhog ceremony of her slain son', the video clip can be seen on YouTube at https://www.youtube.com/watch?v=c9Z5tgt1REw;

CHAPTER 13. THE MAN AND THE SINGER

1. The Red FM Canada interview in available on Youtube at https://www.youtube.com/watch?v=nYr19o6cRWc

2. The interview can be seen on YouTube at https://www. youtube.com/watch?v=jwJ9-U05bU4

3. 'Punjabi singer Sidhu Moose Wala's 5X Fest performance cancelled following police safety assessment', (https://

www.cbc.ca/news/canada/british-columbia/city-of-surrey-forces-cancellation-of-punjabi-rapper-sidhu-moose-wala-s-5x-fest-performance-1.5171099).

4.   'Sidhu Moosewala at The Intersectionality of Market and Punjabi Culture', (https://www.outlookindia.com/national/sidhu-moosewala-at-the-intersectionality-of-market-and-punjabi-culture-news-201720).

5.   Amrit Mann talking about Sidhu Moosewala can be seen on YouTube at https://www.youtube.com/watch?v=1e-xH2u9a0g

CHAPTER 14. MOOSEWALA'S LIFE AND LYRICS

1.   Sidhu Moosewala at Basant Mela Mela Hoshiarpur can be seen on the Doaba TV channel on YouTube at (https://www.youtube.com/watch?v=tAwDxoH4L70&t= 4238s).

2.   'Remembering Sidhu Moosewala: A Transition from Promoting Toxic Masculinity to Becoming a Man with Perceptions',   (https://www.outlookindia.com/national/remembering-sidhu-moosewala-a-transition-from-promoting-toxic-masculinity-to-becoming-a-man-with-perceptions-news-209886).

3.   'Punjab Police book singer Sidhu Moosewala in new case for glorifying gun culture in latest song Sanju', (https://www.hindustantimes.com/cities/punjab-police-book-singer-sidhu-moosewala-in-new-case-for-glorifying-gun-culture-in-latest-song-sanju/story-ov3Uv5fL1Xd0LsEvxCwagJ.html). July 2020

4.   'Sidhu Moose Wala Speaks on Khalistan Licensed Weapons, Exclusive Interview After Jathedar's Statement', the interview can be seen on YouTube at https://www.youtube.com/watch?v=793CowbkYNY. (June 2022)

5. The Red FM Canada interview in available on Youtube at (https://www.youtube.com/watch?v=nYr19o6cRWc). January 2018

6. 'Sidhu Moose Wala Speaks on Khalistan Licensed Weapons, Exclusive Interview After Jathedar's Statement', the interview can be seen on YouTube at (https://www.youtube.com/watch?v=793CowbkYNY.) June 2022

7. 'India has 33.69 lakh gun licences, Uttar Pradesh tops list with 12.77 lakh', (https://www.hindustantimes.com/india-news/india-has-33-69-lakh-gun-licences-uttar-pradesh-tops-list-with-12-77-lakh/story-uRQ9XGCy9wpczOiEMcFmAN.html.) October 2017

8. 'Remembering Sidhu Moosewala: A Transition from Promoting Toxic Masculinity to Becoming a Man with Perceptions', (https://www.outlookindia.com/national/remembering-sidhu-moosewala-a-transition-from-promoting-toxic-masculinity-to-becoming-a-man-with-perceptions-news-209886.)

9. 'How Sidhu Moose Wala's celebration of rural life won him legions of fans in Punjab – and far beyond', https://scroll.in/article/1025431/how-sidhu-moose-walas-celebration-of-rural-life-won-him-legions-of-fans-in-punjab-and-far-beyond.) June 2022

10. 'Gurbani Word Of The Day: baa-bee-haa', from sikh24.com at (https://www.sikh24.com/2017/04/03/gurbani-word-of-the-day-baa-bee-haa/)

11. The discussion can be seen on YouTube at https://www.youtube.com/watch?v=JWqCqbTxi60.

12. 'Remembering Sidhu Moosewala: A Transition From Promoting Toxic Masculinity To Becoming A Man With Perceptions', (https://www.outlookindia.com/national/remembering-sidhu-moosewala-a-transition-from-

promoting-toxic-masculinity-to-becoming-a-man-with-
perceptions-news-209886)

CHAPTER 15: DISPUTES

1.   'How Use Turned to Abuse in Punjab', https://www.
     tribuneindia.com/news/archive/features/how-use-turned-
     to-abuse-in-punjab-31353).

2.   'Drug, drones and death: Inside Punjab's tragic
     stories of addiction', (https://www.newindianexpress.
     com/magazine/2022/oct/30/drug-drones-and-death-
     inside-punjabs-tragic-stories-of-addiction-2512309.
     html#:~:text=Opium%20is%20smuggled%20into%20
     Punjab,in%20Himachal%20Pradesh%20and%20Delhi).

3.   'War on drugs: Challenges for the Punjab government' by
     R.K. Arora and Vinay Kaura, (https://www.orfonline.org/
     research/war-drugs-challenges-punjab-government/).

4.   'It's Official. Drug Abuse Highest in Punjab', (https://
     www.dailypioneer.com/2013/state-editions/its-official-
     drug-abuse-highest-in-punjab.html).

5.   'Life on the brink for families of drug addicts', (https://
     www.tribuneindia.com/news/archive/features/life-on-the-
     brink-for-families-of-drug-addicts-31771). January 2015

6.   'Drug Smuggling Racket: After Dismisaal of AIG Raj Jit
     Singh Punjab Government to Probe Involvement of Other
     SSP Rank Officers', (https://timesofindia.indiatimes.com/
     city/chandigarh/drug-smuggling-racket-after-dismissal-
     of-aig-raj-jit-singh-punjab-govt-to-probe-involvement-of-
     other-ssp-rank-officers/articleshow/99600722.cms)

7.   'Revival of Punjabi cinema - Understanding the dynamics',
     (https://gmj.manipal.edu/issues/december2020/Simran-
     GMJ.pdf)

8. 'Punjab takes centre-stage with its own string of movie hits', (https://www.businesstoday.in/lifestyle/report/story/punjab-film-industry-25697-2011-10-27)

9. 'Drug money in Punjabi films: Actor Mantej Mann arrested in 450-kg drug haul', (https://desibuzzcanada.com/post/drug-money-in-punjabi-films-actor-mantei-mann-arrested-in-450-kg-drug-haul)

10. 'Punjabi Music Industry - The La La Land', (https://tfipost.com/2022/06/punjabi-music-industry-the-la-la-land/)

11. 'Punjab police battles 'drug-taint', (https://www.tribuneindia.com/news/archive/punjab/punjab-police-battles-drug-taint-615877)

12. 'Former Punjab minister and Akali leader Bikram Majithia booked in drugs case', (https://theprint.in/politics/former-punjab-minister-and-akali-leader-bikram-majithia-booked-in-drugs-case/785113/).

13. 'Gangsters gunning for control of Punjab's music industry: Officials', (https://www.hindustantimes.com/india-news/gangsters-gunning-for-control-of-punjab-s-music-industry- officials-see-mumbai-underworld-redux-101658685992259.html)

14. 'Punjabi Music Industry – The La La Land', (https://tfipost.com/2022/06/punjabi-music-industry-the-la-la-land/)

15. 'Bambiha gang investing extortion money in music companies: Mohali SSP', (https://www.hindustantimes.com/cities/chandigarh- news/bambiha-gang-investing-extortion)

16. 'Punjabis contributed to 60% migration to Canada', (https://www.tribuneindia.com/news/jalandhar/punjabis-contributed-to-60-migration-to-canada-44325)

17. 'Asia TV Music Awards 2018: Winners List', https://www.bizasialive.com/britasia-tv-music-awards-2018-winners-list/

CHAPTER 16: THE WAIT FOR JUSTICE

1. 'Moose Wala's neighbour caught trying to flee to Dubai at Amritsar airport' (https://www.hindustantimes.com/cities/chandigarh-news/moose-wala-s-neighbour-caught-trying-to-flee-to-dubai-at-amritsar-airport-101665662916525.html).

2. 'Deepak Tinu, accused in Moosewala murder case, escapes from custody', (https://www.business-standard.com/article/current-affairs/deepak-tinu-accused-in-moosewala-murder-case-escapes-from-custody-122100200654_1.html).

3. 'Gangster Deepak Tinu took 2 months to 'gain' Mansa CIA in-charge's trust', (https://www.hindustantimes.com/cities/chandigarh-news/gangster-deepak-tinu-took-2-months-to-gain-mansa-cia-in-charge-s-trust-101673551546591.html).

CHAPTER 17: ALL THAT IS LEFT BEHIND

1. 'Sidhu Moose Wala murder case: NIA questions Punjabi singers Dilpreet Dhillon and Mankirt Aulakh',(https://www.timesnownews.com/mirror-now/crime/sidhu-moose-wala-murder-case-nia-questions-punjabi-singers-dilpreet-dhillon-and-mankirat-aulakh-article-95278175#:~:text=The%20NIA%20questioned%20Punjabi%20singers,Sidhu%20Moose%20Wala%20murder%20case.)

2. 'Sidhu Moosewala murder accused Sachin Thapan Bishnoi and Anmol Bishnoi detained in Azerbaijan and Kenya: MEA', (https://www.tribuneindia.com/news/punjab/sidhu-moosewala-murder-accused-sachin-thapan-bishnoi-and-anmol-bishnoi-detained-in-azerbaijan-and-kenya-mea-427572).

3. 'Sidhu Moosewala murder accused Anmol Bishnoi spotted with Punjabi singers at wedding event in US; Karan Aujla issues clarification' (https://www.tribuneindia.com/news/trending/sidhu-moosewala-murder-accused-anmol-bishnoi-spotted-with-punjabi-singers-at-wedding-event-in-us-karan-aujla-issues-clarification-498948).

4. Balkaur's video can be seen on YouTube, https://www.youtube.com/watch?v=oHiRCzOBJXY

5. Lawrence Bishnoi's exclusive interview can be seen on YouTube, https://www.youtube.com/watch?v=m_ReWa3xycU

6. Part 2 of Lawrence Bishnoi's exclusive interview can be seen on YouTube, https://www.youtube.com/watch?v=4e9ddzhxytA

7. 'Punjabi singers spread peace message from Dal Lake', (https://www.tribuneindia.com/news/punjab/punjabi-singers-spread-peace-message-from-dal-lake-420499)

8. 'Punjab CM's wife gets security upgrade, now 40 cops to guard her', (https://www.hindustantimes.com/cities/chandigarh-news/punjab-cm-s-wife-gets-security-upgrade-now-40-cops-to-guard-her-101675961360759.html)

ACKNOWLEDGEMENTS

Before I offer my gratitude to the incredible people who played a pivotal role in bringing out this book on the late Sidhu Moosewala, I would like to share that I wish I had written his life story when he was alive. Writing about his death, the result of a gruesome killing, has been a tumultuous and emotional journey.

I am immensely grateful to Mr Rajesh Ramachandran, the editor-in-chief of The Tribune group of publications, for his generous support and encouragement during the writing of this book.

I would like to express my deep appreciation to my literary agent, Jaya Bhattacharji Rose, Ace Literary Consulting, whose unwavering belief in this project and tireless efforts to bring it to life have been invaluable.

I am also grateful to my editors, Sanghamitra, Sanjana, Sonia Madan and Pallavi Mohan for their keen insights, patience and guidance throughout the editorial process. Their commitment to excellence has helped me to shape this book into its best possible form. I would also like to thank Misha Oberoi for the striking cover design.

I extend my heartfelt thanks to my publisher, Westland Books, for taking a chance on my vision and for their support and encouragement every step of the way.

My dear friend Sonia Chauhan deserves special recognition for her constant support and encouragement, her willingness to lend a helping hand whenever I needed it. I would also like to offer my gratitude to a few organisations of writers—Chandigarh Critique Group, Chandigarh Literary Society, The Narrators and the Novel Bunch—which have helped me shape a literary career.

Above all, I owe an enormous debt of gratitude to my wife, Kanchan Vasdev, senior assistant editor with the *Indian Express*. Her unwavering support, encouragement and patience have been the bedrock upon which this book was built. Thank you for giving me the space and time I needed to write, for your motivation, and for being my constant companion and source of inspiration.